DEATH BY DESIGN

DEATH BY DESIGN

The True Story of the Glasgow Necropolis

Ronnie Scott

BLACK & WHITE PUBLISHING

First published 2005
by Black & White Publishing Ltd 99 Giles Street
Edinburgh EH6 6BZ

ISBN 1 84502 047 2

Copyright © Ronnie Scott 2005

The right of Ronnie Scott to be identified as the author
of this work has been asserted by him in accordance with
the Copyright Design and Patents Act 1988.

The line illustrations in the text and the map of
the Necropolis on the inside covers are Copyright© Pol Cavin.

All rights reserved. No part of this publication may be
reproduced, stored in a retrieval system, or transmitted
in any form or by any means, electronic, mechanical,
photocopying, recording or otherwise, without
permission in writing from the Publisher.

A CIP catalogue record is available from
the British Library

Printed and bound by Nørhaven Paperback A/S

Contents

Introduction	xi
1 Building the Silent City	1
2 Pure Dead Brilliant	10
3 On the Tourist Trail	17
4 History Set in Stone	26
5 Making a Grand Exit	32
6 From the Cemetery to the Nursery	42
7 The Bodysnatcher and the Brewer	52
8 It's All Greek to Me	61
9 Ascending towards Heaven	72
10 The Clyde Built Men	85
11 From Common Graves to the Royal Yacht	95
12 All Human Life Is Here	103
13 The Words and the Stones	109
A Short Glossary	116
What Some of the Symbols Mean	120

ACKNOWLEDGEMENTS

Thanks to all my good friends at Hidden Glasgow
(www.hiddenglasgow.com)
and my great field testers –
Andy and Diane, Brian,
Sharon C. and Debbie,
Edward, Jim, Pol, Sharon H.,
Stevie and Tim and Bradley.

REMEMBER, MAN, AS YOU PASS BY,
AS YOU ARE NOW, SO ONCE WAS I:
AS I AM NOW, SO YOU MUST BE,
THEREFORE PREPARE TO FOLLOW ME.

Beneath this, in chalk:

To follow you I'm not content,
Until I know which way you went.

A Word to the Wise

THE WALKING TOUR of the Necropolis is designed for people of average fitness and mobility. Where there are stairs, there are always other paths that will get you there. The Necropolis can be windier and colder than the city centre so dress appropriately.

The author and publisher can take no responsibility for any injuries or other consequences incurred by following the tour given in this book.

This guide is not in any way endorsed by or associated with Glasgow City Council which owns the Glasgow Necropolis.

The epitaphs included here are all to be found in the Glasgow Necropolis.

Introduction

CEMETERIES ARE FOR THE LIVING. Sure, the dead are the permanent residents and the living merely visitors but the Necropolis and every other burying ground in the world were imagined, designed and built by living people for the benefit of other living people. Time, as we are always reminded in graveyards, marches on and one generation of living people is replaced by another, over and over, time without end, amen.

The dead don't care. Buried, burnt, picked over by vultures or left to rot on some battlefield or in some shallow grave, they are beyond caring. It's the living who are shocked and horrified by other people's callous disregard for their loved ones or comforted and given solace by their reverent treatment, happy in the knowledge that the last remains of the dear departed (as the saying goes) are safe and secure in a designated spot where most people will show reverence and respect.

The Glasgow Necropolis gives us a very clear insight into the Victorian cult of the dead, where acres of land were given over to housing hundreds of thousands of pounds' worth of sandstone, granite, marble, cast iron and bronze, all designed and constructed in honour of . . . well, of what? The memory of the dead. The memorialisation of the dead. The monumentation of the dead. By the living and for the living.

Victorian cemeteries were designed to make the living experience particular emotions, to provoke certain philosophical or religious thoughts and to promote certain families and certain ways of life above others. They reflected the values and cultures of the living and not the dead. They reproduced the social structures and the priorities of their times to reinforce these among the living, not the dead.

To visit the Necropolis is to travel back in time, to dip into the Victorian world-view, where the heroes or robber barons (take your pick) of capitalism and the winners and losers of various religious disputes rub shoulders with long-forgotten poets and novelists. It provides a powerful sense of the transience of all things, the fads and fashions that pass into the mists of time, like the Clyde shipyards, the locomotive makers, the shipping lines and the importers of sugar, tea, tobacco and rum.

So, you might ask, how did I become interested in

From duns secure (if creditors should come),
For once, a debtor may be found at home;
By death arrested, and in jail here laid,
The first, the last, the only debt he paid.

Stranger, as you pass o'er this grass,
Think seriously, with no humdrumming;
Prepare for death, for judgment's coming.

all this? Well, after ten years in newspapers and another ten in corporate communications, I wanted a fresh challenge. So I went back to university, muddled through a master's degree in Scottish culture and then imagined I could stand three or four lonely years researching and writing a doctoral thesis. Along the way, I developed an interest in the Necropolis, which is now my topic of study, and found a network of other people interested in the history, meaning and conservation of cemeteries.

I started leading guided tours of the Necropolis. At first they were for fellow students but then they developed into more general gatherings. There are also organised group tours for family historians, medical and surgical people and fans of architecture and the urban environment. Almost everyone I take on my tours has the same three reactions: 'What an amazing place!'; 'Why have I never been here before?'; and 'Surely you should be charging money for this!'. This book is an extension of my tours. It allows readers to take an armchair or a real journey around the Necropolis, and share the same reactions – except the bit about the money, obviously.

Another thing that many people say and which also applies to this book is that having someone show them round, suggesting what they should look out for, explaining the symbols on the tombs or the tombs themselves and offering an insight into the people who are buried there and the people who put them there, makes the experience so much richer. I hope that applies to you.

My enthusiasm for the Necropolis and for introducing as many people as possible to its delights comes from a number of places. Like many Glaswegians, I am intensely proud of my city and the achievements of its people so I get a great feeling showing off this neglected gem to people from outside the city. Another reason is that here we have a fabulous asset that belongs to the people of Glasgow – a real treasure that tells as much about their past as the museums and galleries of the city but which is being lost to the elements and to thoughtless users, day by day.

I would like to see this decline brought to the widest public attention and halted. Not that I want every stone restored to pristine condition, buffed and polished and glinting in the sun, every grave surround put back and fingers, wings and toes glued back on the many fallen angels. The Necropolis is all about death and decay and, if we airbrush that out and create a museum of architecture and sculpture, we are denying these two great constants in life.

Because of this, I am part of the group who are creating the Friends of Glasgow Necropolis, to give a voice to everyone, local or tourist, who has toured the cemetery and quietly thought that this site deserves better. Surely the first garden cemetery in Scotland and a direct descendant of Père Lachaise, the first one in the world, should be an opportunity to show Glasgow in bloom. Surely this grand reflection of Glasgow, at the height of its power and status as Second City of the British Empire, should be inspiring and enthusing young Glaswegians to build better enterprises, think globally and take on the world. Surely the best outdoor sculpture garden in Scotland deserves more cultivated surroundings.

I am not alone in these feelings. Historic Scotland has categorised the landscape and structures of the Necropolis as B-listed and a number of monuments are A-listed, confirming that they are of cultural importance and should be preserved for the enjoyment of generations yet to come. The Necropolis is also listed in the national gardens inventory because of its importance as a designed landscape.

In addition, James Stevens Curl, a pioneer of cemetery studies in these islands, has called the Necropolis 'the most sublime of all British cemeteries'. Ray McKenzie, an undoubted expert on the architectural sculpture of Glasgow and the author of the definitive study on this subject, has declared that:

> the Necropolis should long ago have been designated a National Treasure . . . it unfolds as a succession of architectural and sculptural gems unrivalled almost anywhere in the world, even by the celebrated Père Lachaise cemetery in Paris, on which it was partly modelled.

The Necropolis is already mentioned in most of the tourist guidebooks to Glasgow, Scotland and the United Kingdom and it is well signposted on the internet for family-history researchers. As leisure travel changes and cultural tourism, roots tourism and even dark tourism increase in importance, both generally in the world and specifically as of potential economic benefit for Glasgow, the Necropolis looks more and more like a wasted opportunity for the city and its people.

In case you've not been following recent trends in leisure travel, here are some rough definitions.

Cultural tourism is people travelling to see museums, galleries, monuments and buildings, as well as shops, restaurants and clubs, rather than sun, sea, sand and, er, sangria. Roots tourism is people visiting countries and cities to see where their ancestors lived, worked and were buried. Dark tourism is people travelling to sites connected with death and disaster, from burial grounds to the plaza in Dallas where President John F. Kennedy was killed. This can vary from the tasteful to the tasteless. If you spent a break in Paris visiting Père Lachaise, Le Pantheon and Les Invalides (where Napoleon's tomb lies), few would bat an eyelid; add the Catacombs and the underground sewer museum and you're heading towards being talked about behind your back (guess where I've been in Paris).

Given that Glasgow has put culture and tourism at the heart of its economic regeneration, the Necropolis is an opportunity too good to miss. Regardless of who created and paid for it – rather like the Burrell Collection and the treasures of Kelvingrove – it is now part of our common heritage and deserves to be treated as such. This is the challenge facing the Friends of Glasgow Necropolis.

For more information, please visit:
   www.glasgownecropolis.org

I hope this book conveys some of my enthusiasm for the Glasgow Necropolis and I hope it and your tour help you to become as intrigued, interested and inspired by it as I am.

Please take care when in the Necropolis, as surfaces can be uneven and grassy paths slippery, especially when wet. Monuments can become unsteady so don't lean on them and don't put yourself in the way of a monument that someone else could lean on. A very small number of people are injured in Scottish burial grounds each year but, by taking these simple precautions, you will not be among them. Always follow the advice in the Historic Scotland guide on visitor safety in cemeteries, which is available online (www.historic-scotland.gov.uk). That said, enjoy your visit to the Necropolis.

The on-line companion to this book is at:
   www.glasgownecropolis.com.

For Bill and Nancy Scott

1
BUILDING THE SILENT CITY

THE GLASGOW NECROPOLIS is a time capsule – a way of directly experiencing the city at the height of its industrial power and commercial might, when it was the Second City of the British Empire.

Although many of their names have passed from memory, the people buried here and the monuments raised to them have a lasting resonance – they were the men and women who built the Victorian city we can see from the summit of the Necropolis. They are the merchants, the shipbuilders, the iron-founders, the architects and the engineers who built the wealth of Glasgow. They are the lawyers and preachers, the accountants and doctors, the Lord Provosts and professors who moulded the city and gave it its character.

The Glasgow Necropolis was amongst the first of the great cemeteries of the British Isles and is roughly contemporary with St James's Cemetery in Liverpool (which opened in 1829), Glasnevin Cemetery in

Dublin (1832) and the General Cemetery of All Souls, Kensal Green, in London (1833). Glasgow's new cemetery opened for business in May 1833. With the cemetery's development, an uneconomic site on the edge of the city was turned into a lucrative enterprise that quickly became a fashionable place to be seen for both the living and the dead.

The story began five years earlier, in the house of James Ewing, who had been Dean of Guild of the Merchants' House and would soon be Lord Provost and one of the city's MPs. Dean of Guild was the title given to the person elected president of the Merchants' House. The post-holder held the title for two years. In July 1828, Ewing hosted a meeting of some of the senior figures in the Merchants' House which represented the traders and businesspeople of Glasgow and which owned the Fir Park, overlooking the Cathedral. At this meeting, they discussed a proposal, made by Laurence Hill, the Collector of the Merchants' House, to convert the Fir Park into a grand cemetery, modelled on Père Lachaise in Paris. The committee unanimously recommended the proposal to the Merchants' House. Members of the committee drew up a full proposal and, in October

1829, the House accepted it. In January 1831, the House advertised for plans to be submitted and the sixteen responses it got were put on public display. No single competition entry was chosen but three advisers to the Merchants' House – Stewart Murray, the curator of the Botanic Garden, and the architects David Hamilton and John Baird – drew up a plan that combined the best elements of the five winning ones.

In 1832, George Milne, a landscape gardener, was appointed as superintendent and asked to lay out the grounds under the direction of those three wise men. The Merchants' House built the impressive gateway to the Necropolis, the gatekeeper's lodge, the superintendent's lodge, the handsome bridge connecting the Cathedral precinct with the Necropolis, the structure known as The Façade at the east end of the bridge and the Egyptian Vaults. The statue to John Knox had been constructed in 1825, three years before the meeting in Ewing's house, on a site which Glasgow historian George Eyre-Todd, writing in 1934, stated was used by sun-worshippers in pre-Christian times. Given the Glasgow weather, they would have been sun-worshippers with umbrellas.

All through this process, John Strang, a journalist and critic who later became the City Chamberlain of Glasgow, had published articles in various newspapers, setting out the arguments for a grand cemetery, modelled on Père Lachaise. It would be completely different from the crowded and unhygienic churchyards of Glasgow and suitable both for sanitary burial and civilised mourning. In 1831, he published *Necropolis Glasguensis*, which surveyed funeral and burial customs in older cultures and other countries and suggested how a grand ornamental cemetery could be built in Glasgow.

The book included a description and sketch of Père Lachaise in Paris and a frontispiece illustrating how the Fir Park could look if the Merchants' House followed his advice. In it, Strang began with the current condition of Scottish churchyards, which he thought were 'generally neglected' and in a 'melancholy state'. He argued – in a typical nineteenth-century wordy and flowery manner – for an ornamental cemetery 'at once respectful to the dead and safe and sanatory (*sic*) to the living' which would also be 'peculiarly dedicated to the genius of memory and calculated for the extension of religious and moral feelings'. His plan would make burying grounds 'more an ornament and less a nuisance', he argued.

Strang's ideas were remarkably in tune with those of the Merchants' House for the Necropolis did become much more than a public health project, with memory and morals high on the agenda. He proposed four regulations for the cemetery and these were, to varying degrees, adopted by the house. Strang's regulations were:

1. The Necropolis should be non-denominational.
2. Its memorials must be approved by the House.
3. Plots should be at least sixteen feet broad.
4. The cemetery should be overseen by a gardener.

The Scotsman welcomed the book, suggesting that, because of the amount of facts and detail crammed into its sixty-four pages, it should be retitled *The Gravediggers' Manual*. Its reviewer, who had also visited Père Lachaise, hoped that the people of Glasgow had enough 'sense, taste and fancy' to support the

Merchants' House plan for the Fir Park. Strang's book became the blueprint for how people saw the Necropolis, as a modern-day equivalent of the tasteful and hygienic burying grounds of classical Greece and Rome, and it was viewed as a handbook for how they should behave and feel when they were in it.

There were two burials before the official opening. The first was that of **Joseph Levi**, who was interred in September 1832 in the plot that Glasgow's small Jewish community had purchased in 1830. And the second person to be buried there was **Elizabeth Miles**, the stepmother of the superintendent, who was laid to rest in February 1833.

Within the Necropolis, the internal arrangements can be seen to mirror the social or class distinctions of the city in the nineteenth century. Only the truly elite were allowed to be buried on the summit of the hill, near to the monument to John Knox. The cream of the commercial crop and the middle classes were distinguished by the size and prominence of their memorials. The poor continued to be buried in unmarked graves and the members of the Jewish community had their own demarcated spot.

The geographical boundaries and restrictions on size are also reflected in the scale of charges, printed as part of the first regulations in 1834. Lairs cost two guineas (£2.10) a square yard (roughly equivalent to a square metre) at the top of the hill and one guinea (£1.05) lower down. There were four classes of adult funerals, which corresponded to the social positions and wealth of families: when the body is carried on a hearse, drawn by four horses or shoulder high, two guineas (£2.10); when the body is carried on a hearse, drawn by two horses, one guinea (£1.05); when the body is carried on handspokes, accompanied by two or more ushers, 15 shillings (75p); and when the body is carried on handspokes, without ushers, five shillings (25p). The costs of digging graves and erecting memorials were over and above this.

By 1877, the whole enterprise had become such a success that the Necropolis was extended that year and again in 1892, by which time it had reached its present extent of 17 acres (15 hectares). However, with the rise of suburban cemeteries, the popularity of the Necropolis declined and, in 1966, it was handed over to the Corporation of Glasgow (now Glasgow City Council) along with a sum of £50,000 towards its upkeep.

From visual evidence, it is easy to see the Necropolis as solely an elite burying ground since the

As on this spot I drew my infant breath,
Here let me rest when I repose in death;
And when the last trump's pealing notes shall sound,
Oh! May our lot among the blest be found.

(on the tomb of James Mitchell, who was buried on the site of the house his father and grandfather lived in)

3,500 tombs commemorate the well-off, whether they were merchants or tradespeople, ministers or military leaders. But there are 50,000 people interred here, meaning that the majority of the people who call the Necropolis home were ordinary folk, who were charged ordinary prices and who were buried safely and securely in communal graves with no headstones. Their details, of course, were entered in the burial records alongside those of the better-off. So, if your ancestor was among either of these groups, it's possible to find out more about them from these records. All of the records of the Necropolis are in the care of Glasgow City Council and are to be found in one of three places – the Glasgow Archives, the Mitchell Library or the Cemeteries and Crematoria Department. The Archives have the records of the Merchants' House, which trace the story of the construction and operation of the Necropolis from 1828 to 1966. The Mitchell Library has burial registers from 1832 to the present, including an indexed transcript of all the burials during the years 1832–54. And the Cemeteries and Crematoria Department has the lair records and maps from 1832 to the present.

2
PURE DEAD BRILLIANT

THE NECROPOLIS WAS a significant improvement in Glasgow, both from the point of public health and moral sentiment. As a civic amenity, it was, as the cemetery historian James Stevens Curl noted, 'the first major cemetery in Scotland . . . in terms of hygiene and sanitation' which also 'inaugurated a new era in Glasgow and set an example to other towns which was speedily followed throughout the country'. The Necropolis was also intended to provide moral improvement. The Merchants' House intended that its cemetery would be both an attractively designed and built burying ground and an ornamental park for both walking and contemplating. The monuments and memorial inscriptions – all of which had to meet with their approval – were designed to instruct and inspire the visiting citizens.

These views were also expressed by George Blair who, in his book *Biographic and Descriptive Sketches of the Necropolis* which was published in 1857, noted that 'we go to epitaphs for useful lessons, and we meditate amid the tombs for improvement'. Blair's enthusiasm for the morally uplifting properties of the Necropolis reflects the views of the Merchants' House. He wrote that:

> Many individuals who would never otherwise have known that such men existed in this great city, and acted a conspicuous and useful part in the world, are thus made acquainted with their history and their worth, and are inspired with a laudable ambition to imitate and emulate their example. This must be especially the case when a visit to the monuments and resting-places of the dead is rendered attractive to the public.

So the monuments of the Necropolis became a grandiose collective advertisement for mercantile capitalism. As Alexander Welsh, in his student dissertation on the Necropolis for The Mackintosh School of Architecture, wrote, the monuments also showed how the merchant classes 'aspired to the standards of traditional society . . . and raised impressive memorials to themselves, emulating in scale and richness the family tombs of country estates anywhere'.

The designs of these memorials were subject to strict scrutiny by the Merchants' House. For example, applicants for plots in 1834 were instructed to 'erect handsome and ornamental architectural buildings and dress and maintain the lots agreeably to the plans and in the way pointed out and represented to them'. The regulations of the Necropolis insisted that no 'mason work or monument' or any inscriptions thereon can be carried out until they have been 'submitted to the Merchants' House, and received its approbation'. The regulations also laid down strict rules for the maintenance of monuments and the suppression of 'weeds and rank grass' and stipulated a fine of five shillings (25p) for visitors who walk on anything but the prescribed path.

In the early days of the Necropolis, the Merchants' House was keen to encourage memorials designed and built to high standards and preferred them to be sited on prominent areas that were visible from the surrounding streets. The best sites were sold more expensively. One of the premium positions was the area around the John Knox memorial and designs for proposed tombs in that area were submitted for approval to Thomas Hamilton, who had designed the towering memorial to the Scots reformer.

The Necropolis was widely welcomed. There was great demand to purchase lairs, to bury important family members there and to build monuments to people who were buried elsewhere. The social cachet associated with the Necropolis was shown by the cemetery historian James Stevens Curl who wrote that 'nearly every eminent Glaswegian who had died between 1832 and 1867 was either interred within the Necropolis or was represented by a cenotaph'. This practice led George Blair to call the Necropolis 'the Westminster Abbey of Glasgow'.

Victorian Valhalla or not, the Necropolis was multi-denominational. Neoclassical – which could also be seen as pre-Christian – inspiration was sought for the name of the cemetery, the predominant architectural styles and the compartments into which the cemetery was divided. And while St James's in Liverpool and All Souls in London took Christian titles, Glasgow took the Classical path. It was not the first burying ground in the British Isles to adopt the word Necropolis, however, as it was used from 1825 in Liverpool, although for a far smaller cemetery.

The range of styles of monuments also demonstrates a move away from the traditions of the established church and perhaps even of Christianity itself. As Curl noted, the Necropolis contains 'every style of architectural monument, from purest Greek to

Our little lambs, which promised fair,
To us but short were given;
But they have made a happy change,
From this vain world to heaven.

(on a family tomb that records
the death of five children)

dissenting Gothic, and from chaste slab to Moresque mausoleum'. The monuments were admired by almost everyone in Glasgow. Almost everyone, that is, with the exception of J. F. S. Gordon, priest of St Andrew's Episcopalian Church on Glasgow Green. He complained of 'weak and fulsome epitaphs' on stones surmounted by 'towels, tea-caddies and soup-tureens, thus carrying the marks of the shop even here'. All this was unchristian, he wrote, since it recalled 'how pagans of old burnt their dead and kept their ashes in urns and vases'. His rant even extended to modern coffins which he said were 'bespattered with tinsel heads, having wings and puffy piper-cheeks lustily blowing bugle horns'. More tea, vicar?

So what was the situation in Glasgow before the coming of the Necropolis in 1833? In the period between the census years 1801 and 1831, the city nearly tripled in population, from 77,385 to 202,426, and the area around Glasgow Cross had become an overcrowded and filthy slum. The city burying grounds were struggling to keep up with rising numbers of corpses, which rose dramatically when disease, such as the cholera epidemic of 1832, swept through the city. The burying grounds were pretty much restricted to the areas around the Cathedral, which was substantially extended to the north in 1800, and the Ramshorn Church, which had been extended in 1780. These burying grounds were filling up rapidly and coffins were often buried with just a few inches of earth above them, sometimes with horrific consequences. Public health considerations aside, churchyards were no place to linger and contemplate the lives of the dear departed, whether during funerals or on later visits to the graveside.

There was also the little matter of grave robbing. Medical education was booming in Glasgow in the opening decades of the nineteenth century, both at the university and in private medical schools, and there was a ready market for anatomical subjects with no questions asked regarding their provenance. As well as exhuming bodies in Glasgow and the surrounding areas, traders in corpses imported cadavers from Dublin, boxed and salted. Although the Anatomy Act of 1832 was designed to put a stop to all that, fears lingered and the Necropolis regulations specified that all graves should be securely sealed.

3

ON THE TOURIST TRAIL

THE GLASGOW NECROPOLIS quickly became a tourist attraction, featuring in the city guidebooks from the year of its opening and having its own tourist handbook by 1836. The Merchants' House was forced to employ a gatekeeper to supervise the rapidly increasing number of visitors, including those from America and around the world. The gatekeeper was responsible for making sure that everyone entering the cemetery, except as part of a funeral, signed the visitors' book. One page from an early visitors' book, with some of the entries for 23 and 24 June 1835, shows the large number and wide range of people who were attracted to the Necropolis. This one page shows thirty-six visitors – eleven from Glasgow and the rest from as far afield as Belfast, Dublin, Manchester, London, New York and Boston. By 1836, there were more than 100 visitors each day and, by 1839, the minutes of the Merchants' House recorded that the Necropolis had 'acquired a celebrity unequalled by any similar establishment in the United Kingdom and is daily resorted to by vast numbers of visitors including strangers from every part of the globe'.

Back in 1828, Laurence Hill, one of the founders of the Necropolis, and James Ewing, at whose home the meeting to establish the new cemetery was held, both predicted that the Necropolis would become a 'general resort'. Given that Scottish graveyards at that time were muddy, overcrowded and often quite smelly places, this must have seemed like a very unusual thing to believe but the ensuing huge public interest in this new civic amenity proved them both correct. Andrew Aird was one of several Glasgow men who, in the latter part of the nineteenth century, wrote their memoirs, many of these memoirs capturing the feel of the city perfectly. Writing as an old man in his book *Glimpses of Old Glasgow* of 1894, Aird looked back to the early days of the cemetery and recalled that 'the Necropolis was ... what it still is, one of the favourite resorts of strangers'.

A writer in *The Scots Times* showed a German visitor round the Necropolis in August 1835. He reported:

> On Thursday last we had the pleasure of visiting it along with M. von Raumer, the celebrated Professor of History at Berlin, and although he had visited and recollected the general appearance of almost all the cemeteries in Europe, he declared that to few of them would our Necropolis yield in picturesque beauty, and to still fewer in romantic effect.

Laurence Hill published the booklet *A Companion to the Necropolis* in 1836. This thirty-six-page guide was sold, according to the guide itself, by booksellers in Glasgow, Edinburgh and London and 'at the gates of the Necropolis', which showed that it had a ready market, both for the prospective traveller and the curious local. This first guidebook helped people to understand the landscape and monuments of the Necropolis and it used the ideas of beauty, contemplation and memory as ways of interpreting the cemetery.

Another visitor who admired the appearance of the Necropolis was Christian Ployen, the Danish-born commandant of the Faroe Islands. When Ployen visited Scotland in the summer of 1839, he passed briefly through Glasgow and was shown round by a Mr Drysdale, a seedsman to whom he had a letter of introduction. Ployen had time to visit only five places chosen by his host – a cotton factory, the Royal Exchange, the Cathedral, the Necropolis and the Argyll Arcade – which shows that the Necropolis was in the top-five visitor attractions within six years of opening.

William McPhun's 1840 guide to the city set the Necropolis firmly in the same class of attraction as the Cathedral, the Royal Exchange, Glasgow University and the Hunterian Museum and the Zoological Gardens. McPhun described the Necropolis as both visually appealing and morally uplifting – and, in a typical Glasgow manner, free of charge:

> From the advantageous situation of this burying place, being principally placed on the front of the hill, it is a great ornament to this part of the city ... If the stranger's time admits of it, an hour or two may be most agreeably and profitably spent in traversing the fine walks here and looking around him on the *mementi* (*sic*) *mori* that surround him. Admittance gratuitous from dawn to dusk.

The twin aspects of the Necropolis, as being both beautiful and inspiring, are also seen in the guide to the Cathedral and the Necropolis written by Peter

Buchan in the early 1840s. This pocket-sized book offered a twenty-four-page guided tour of the Necropolis and ended with two pages headed 'Fees payable for interments in the Necropolis', presumably for the benefit of those travellers considering a second, much longer, visit. Buchan's guide to 'this palace of the triumphant dead' noted that 'a more picturesque spot could not have been chosen for a Père Lachaise after the model of the one in Paris' and that it had 'an air of melancholy gloom, suited to the subject and place'. Ideal place for a picnic, then.

John Claudius Loudon, one of the most significant figures in British garden design in the first half of the nineteenth century, published a long review and commentary on the Necropolis in *The Gardener's Magazine* in 1842. He wrote that 'the impression made by the first view of this hill, studded with trees and tombs and scars of solid rock, when looking from the town, with the Cathedral in the foreground, is grand and melancholy'. The Scots-born Loudon wrote that the bridge over the Molendinar linked the Cathedral churchyard with the Necropolis and someone standing on the bridge, 'looking down on one cemetery and up towards the other, has his mind filled with the subject to the exclusion of every other idea and feels, in short, the effect on his mind to be sublime'.

Gardening authority Loudon, a sort of combined Sir Roy Strong and Alan Titchmarsh of his day, was impressed by the quality of the monuments. He approved that the majority of the memorials were in architectural forms, rather than having 'the mean appearance of being thrust in like stakes or laid down like pavement' and had lettering either well cut in the stone 'or raised in metallic forms', which 'ought not to be neglected when an architectural character is to be maintained'.

George Blair, who wrote *Biographic and Descriptive Sketches of Glasgow Necropolis* in 1857, was certainly impressed by the cemetery, which he called 'a silent but significant city of the dead'. His guidebook helped fuel the importance of the Necropolis as a visitor attraction and as an appropriate burying place for the great and the good, who were celebrated in his writing. Blair showed great enthusiasm for the morally uplifting properties of the Necropolis.

J. A. Hammerton, writing in the 1890s, offered a guided 'tour of inspection' of the Necropolis in his book *Sketches from Glasgow*. He began with the

MOTHER
WEEP NOT FOR ME; BUT BE
YOU ALSO READY.

KEEP SAFE THESE TREASURES, CHEST OF CLAY,
TILL THEY ARE CALLED FOR AT THE
JUDGMENT DAY;
FOR WHILE THESE JEWELS HERE ARE SET,
THE GRAVE IS BUT THEIR CABINET.

(on the graves of two children)

Bridge of Sighs, noting that the original bridge of that name, in Venice, linked the Doge's Palace and the town prison. Hammerton confessed that, in the Glasgow version, he was never sure whether the city or the Necropolis represented the prison or the palace. Hammerton was sure of one thing, though. In the preface to his book he stated flatly, 'Glasgow is one of the most interesting places in the universe.'

Gardeners and writers of guidebooks may have found the Necropolis interesting but it was the poets who were able to express how it felt to be there. A poem 'by a lady', published in the *Glasgow Herald* in 1834, dealt with the recurring themes of the beauties of garden cemeteries compared to overcrowded churchyards, the contemplation of death and mortality and the commemoration of the good and great. To the modern reader, these poems are inordinately tedious so there will be no quotations – be thankful, be very thankful!

Lydia Huntley Sigourney, an American poet who visited Glasgow in 1839, was inspired by her tour of the Necropolis to put quill to parchment. Her poem, 'The Necropolis at Glasgow', was published in Boston in 1842. Other, more local poets were quick to follow suit in praise of the cemetery. For example, Hugh

Brown, an Ayrshire poet who visited the Necropolis during the first ten years of its existence, published 'Lines, on Visiting the Glasgow Necropolis', in 1844.

Even today, in a secular society where death is kept from public view, the Necropolis is a popular tourist attraction.

4
History Set in Stone

THE NECROPOLIS attracts hordes of family historians, desperate for that middle name or elusive birth date that will turn out to be the missing piece in their complex jigsaw and finally prove their family connection to William Wallace, King Robert the Bruce, Sir Walter Scott or Wee Jimmy Krankie.

Natural historians, too, are interested in the flora and fauna that thrive in this green oasis in the heart of the city. As you might expect, the Necropolis is home to foxes, rabbits, bats, birds and other small animals. There have also been sightings of roe deer but no explanation about how they might have got there. One version is that they were pets belonging to a family in a block of flats but were put out just before they were too big to fit in the lift. But that's maybe just a story. Anyway, deer don't like lifts.

Here we come to a bit of a disagreement. The family folk want to read the inscriptions on gravestones but the flora folk don't like people tampering with the lichen and other rudimentary life forms that enjoy living on old stone. Some of them are hundreds of years old (that's the lichen, not their admirers) and can give clues about the environment and weather down the centuries.

There are other disagreements, too. People with an overriding interest in heath and safety would like to see all the monuments laid flat so that no one can be injured by falling stones. Everyone else thinks that the beauty of our cemeteries would be ruined by this. There's another argument here – the conservationists advocate that the stones, once toppled, be properly bedded and insulated from the soil so that ground water doesn't ruin the fabric. They would prefer these monuments to be face down, keeping the inscriptions safe from the big boots and even bigger lawnmowers of cemetery workers. You can imagine the howls from the family history people.

The other groups who have a vested interest in cemeteries are the art and architectural historians, who are fascinated by individual stones (but only the nice ones), and the historians, who see the whole cemetery as an open book to be read and interpreted, to enrich our knowledge of times and people past. All of these special interest groups have something to add to our understanding and enjoyment of the Necropolis, even if their competing agendas mean they don't always agree about the best way of looking after this great asset.

The Necropolis is also a magnet for creative types. The films *Deathwatch* (aka *La Mort en direct*) (Bertrand Tavernier, 1980) and *Wilbur Wants to Kill Himself* (Lone Scherfig, 2002) included powerful scenes shot there, taking advantage of both the ambiance of the Necropolis and the dramatic views over the city from the summit. Another artistic work that borrowed the Necropolis as a dark backdrop for its story is *The Bogie Man*, a fabulous graphic novel written by John Wagner and Alan Grant and illustrated by Robin Smith.

Alasdair Gray, that Scottish national treasure, imagined the Necropolis as the entry into an underground Glasgow in his great novel *Lanark*, where the hero is swallowed by a huge mouth while walking in the Necropolis and awakes to find himself in The Institute. I'm waiting for the movie, myself.

Lawrence Russell and Rick 'Ajo' McGrath have written a film treatment which involves 'two Canadian media thugs' – who bear no resemblance whatsoever to the authors, oh no – travelling to Glasgow in search of the missing ashes of Alexander Trocchi, heroin addict, author of *Young Adam* and fringe member of both the Beats and the Situationists. They trawl the Necropolis for clues. Oddly, that one hasn't made it to the silver screen.

Artists, too, have found the Necropolis fascinating, with a number of painters, such as Michael Murray, producing canvases of the monuments and their environment. And students from the Glasgow School of Art are frequently to be seen, sketchbook in hand, surveying the monuments (and not always just the nice ones). Student stonemasons from Glasgow Metropolitan College and people on continuing education classes at Strathclyde University can also be seen following their tutors around the headstones.

During the first annual BLOCK: Architecture Festival in 2004, two twilight tours of the Necropolis were hugely oversubscribed by people wanting to learn about the monuments and the people buried below them. Other tours are held regularly by a number of people and groups, including the New Glasgow Society, park rangers employed by the city council and (ahem) yours truly. Other groups who have a particular fondness for the Necropolis are

Caer Clud, a druid group which has performed ceremonies there, the Scottish Vampyre Society which has – no, on second thoughts, you don't really want to know what they get up to – and the denizens of Hidden Glasgow, a website for aficionados of the lesser-trodden paths of the city, who have taken and posted many fine photographs of the silent city.

The newly formed Friends of Glasgow Necropolis also have, strangely enough, an interest in the place and time will tell what influence they have over maintenance and conservation, not to mention in increasing visitor numbers and giving people more knowledge and understanding of the site.

Now, our grand tour of the Necropolis begins . . .

What joy when she resigned her breath,
For as her eyelids closed, she smiled in death.

(to a wife from her husband)

Happy innocents! We fell,
Like flowers before the reaper,
Weep not if thou lov'st us well,
We're happier than the weeper.

(on the grave of a child)

5
MAKING A GRAND EXIT

CARLO GINZBURG, an Italian historian, has written that 'the attempt to gain knowledge of the past is also a journey into the world of the dead'. That's a pretty concise summing up of what this tour of the Necropolis, contained in this and the following seven chapters, is all about. We're going to explore Victorian Glasgow, through the lives and monuments of its former inhabitants.

Just as they were dynamic and purposeful during their lives, these long-dead Glaswegians made a big impact when they came to the end of them. No more the muddy churchyard and a few hardy friends around the coffin – they demanded black-plumed horses drawing elaborate hearses, crowds and speeches at the grave and a large architect-designed stone to remind the passers-by just how important they had been. In short, they wanted to make a grand exit and the Necropolis was there to allow them to do that.

There was very little ceremony involved in a funeral at the burying grounds of Glasgow before the Necropolis. This was partly because the Reformation had downgraded the importance of funerals, partly because churchyards were pretty simple in their layout and entrances and partly because, at least by the early nineteenth century, these burial grounds were filled to overflowing and not the nicest place to hang around.

The Necropolis, in great contrast, was hygienic and attractively laid out and it had strict quotas on the number of burials in each lair. Improved hygiene was brought about by the installation of a system of drains, unknown in any earlier churchyard, and it was promoted by the effect of the wind swirling around such an exposed hill. The design and planting system gave the Necropolis the look of well-tended grounds around a grand country house, rather than a muddy burying ground in the heart of a city. The impressive gates at the entrance to the Necropolis and the sweeping grand drive across the bridge and into the cemetery provided a suitably imposing setting for the transition from the city of the living to the city of the dead. The perfect place, then, for making that grand exit.

Our tour begins at the imposing entrance gates of the Necropolis, at the south-east corner of the Cathedral precinct. If this entrance is closed, which it is at weekends and on public holidays, then follow the modern building to the right of the gates round the corner and into Cathedral Square where there is a far less impressive entrance at number 52, opposite the Cathedral House Hotel.

The first three structures to take note of are the entrance gates, the gatekeeper's lodge and the superintendent's lodge. The first of these, designed in 1838 by David and James Hamilton, features the crest of the Merchants' House of Glasgow, the original developer of the Necropolis, in the centre of each leaf. They were manufactured by Thomas Edington and Sons, of the Phoenix Iron Works, Garscube, Glasgow. They also celebrate William Brown of Kilmardinny, the Dean of Guild at the time they were designed. The gatekeeper's lodge, also designed by David and James Hamilton, was built in a neo-Norman style in 1839. This was originally the office of the superintendent and it also housed the gatekeeper, who made sure that everyone signed the visitors' book. The superintendent's lodge is a later construction, built in 1890 in a vaguely Tudor style.

A modern addition to these structures is a small area set aside for parents to mourn the loss of their very young children. There are no graves or scattered ashes here, just a place for quiet contemplation.

As you walk east towards the bridge, look to your left into the Cathedral burying ground and notice that parts of the wall have been removed and replaced by iron railings. This was done by the Merchants' House, with the assistance of the Town Council, in the 1830s to give mourners and visitors a visual reminder that the new cemetery was strongly linked to the heritage and values of the ancient High Church.

Just before you step on to the bridge, look for the fixings in the ground where the grand entrance gates used to be, before they were moved to the west after the Barony church was demolished in 1890. The gatekeeper's lodge was originally just inside this gate, to the left where the railings now are.

The Bridge of Sighs, designed by David and James Hamilton in 1833, originally carried Necropolis traffic over the Molendinar Burn, which was especially wide at this point because of the mill pond for the Subdean Mill, which stood roughly where the top of Ladywell Street is now. If you look south from the bridge and look down to your left, you can see a gate into the Necropolis, with a cul-de-sac behind it. That's Ladywell Street. The Subdean Mill is long gone but the Molendinar Burn, which provided the power to drive the mill, is still here. However, it was conducted into a buried pipe and Wishart Street was built along its course in 1877.

In the early days of the Necropolis, the journey over the Molendinar reminded many Christians of the River Jordan, which separates the wilderness of the world from the Promised Land. Others were reminded of the River Styx which, in Greek mythology, flowed between this world and Hades, the underworld. To cross from one bank to the other, the dead had to pay Charon, the ferryman. The River Lethe also flowed in Hades and any of the residents who drank from it lost all memory of their life on earth. If the Necropolis is Hades and the Molendinar is the Styx, then maybe the brewery round the corner can stand in for the Lethe.

The foundation stone for the bridge was laid with much ceremony in October 1834, when James Hutchison, the Dean of Guild, as President of the Merchants' House, made an effusive speech and James Ewing, the Lord Provost, replied in an equally flowery way. Some appropriate musical accompaniment was provided by the band of the Cathedral and students from local schools. The Dean of Guild said that the bridge linked people of 'this commercial city' with the 'silent but interesting city of the dead' and he hoped that, when the Necropolis was completed, it would, together with the Cathedral, 'form a scene so magnificent and so interesting as will scarcely be equalled by any thing (*sic*) of the kind in the United Kingdom'. No modesty, there, then.

In reply, the Lord Provost noted that the Molendinar should remind everyone present of 'the river which we must all cross – the separation between time and eternity'. And, just as the gaps in the churchyard wall were intended to connect the Necropolis with the Cathedral in people's minds, the bridge was repeatedly described by both as a physical and metaphorical link between the ancient church and the new cemetery.

Alexander Hamilton, an American Baptist minister, visited the Necropolis in 1848. He wrote: 'A bold and splendid arch spans the Molendinar Burn, whose waters, when collected into a small dam or lake, dash violently over an artificial cascade, down a steep ravine, affording a sort of melancholy cheerfulness to the scenes around us.' An early incarnation of the Reverend I. M. Jolly, it would seem.

When you get a chance, look at the bridge from the side and you will see three archways. The central span is a dramatic eighteen-metre Roman semi-circular arch, which vaulted the wide millpond of the Molendinar. The small arch on the Necropolis side, now almost totally obscured by undergrowth, allowed the millrace to flow from the millpond to the Subdean Mill. And the archway on the west side, being wide enough for a horse and cart, gave access from the town to the North Washing Green, just north of the Cathedral. There, members of the North Washing Green Society could wash their clothes in the Molendinar and hang them up to dry – a sort of outdoor steamie.

Continue walking across the bridge and stop when you are in the turning circle, which gave room for horse-drawn hearses to turn on their way in and out of the Necropolis. The sandstone edifice facing you has not had a happy history. The Façade, as it is known, was designed in 1836 by John Bryce to fulfil three functions. These were:

1. to be an ornamental entrance to the Necropolis;
2. to provide six burial vaults;
3. to be the imposing entrance to grand catacombs.

The catacombs were planned to be vast burial chambers set deep in the rock. They would have come off a central tunnel that was to have been blasted through the hill to the quarry beyond.

Four of the six burial vaults that can be seen in the concave face of the building were never sold and these have been expertly concreted up. The other two vaults faced each other on the inside of the tunnel, just behind where the black doors are. That was the plan. However, the hill collapsed when tunnelling began, the builder ran out of money, the vaults filled up with water and nobody wanted to be buried in the dark hillside when they could spend eternity in a pleasant garden beneath a huge stone advertisement for themselves.

The Façade, which includes an inscription in moulded bronze that was once attached to the bridge, is now in a sorry state, with entrances to the burial vaults filled in and the big black doors leading to

The Façade, designed by John Bryce.

nothing more exciting than the city council's collection of big lawnmowers. At one point, before the opening of the Egyptian Vaults, it was used as a temporary shelter for coffins while their owners were having their graves prepared. Above the doors is a badly eroded crest, probably that of the Merchants' House.

Architects disagree about the style of this concave structure, which has been variously described as Italian Mannerist, Jacobean, Elizabethan and Roman Gothic – take your pick. Whatever it is, the architects of The Façade (John Bryce) and the nearby bridge (the firm of David and James Hamilton) were responsible for some of the most prominent monuments in the Necropolis. William Barr has written that around three quarters of the remainder were produced by the firm of John and George Mossman, the city's pre-eminent architectural sculptors and monumental masons.

Still facing The Façade, turn to your left and take the descending path to the left of the main carriageway. This will bring you along the inside of the perimeter railings and, at the end of this path, there is an enclosed area with a tall stone pillar. This is the Jewish cemetery, where the first burial in the Necropolis took place in September 1832.

6
FROM THE CEMETERY TO THE NURSERY

THIS SECTION OF THE WALK takes us from the Jewish cemetery, where the first burial took place, to the monument of a man who was buried elsewhere.

'The first land-marks (*sic*) of a community of Jews are a synagogue and a cemetery,' wrote Abraham Levy, an early historian of that community in Glasgow. Once the synagogue had been established, the construction of the Necropolis gave the Jews of Glasgow an ideal chance to buy a communal plot, rather than have to do what they had been doing up to this point and transport their dead to Edinburgh.

The Jewish community paid 100 guineas (£105) to the Merchants' House for the cemetery, which included the land, the wall around it and the ornamental column and gateway, which were designed in consultation with the community. John Bryce designed the column, in an Assyrian style, and John Park designed the gateway and scrolled arch. The cast-iron gate, now missing, was made at the Phoenix Iron Works.

At the top of the column are the Hebrew initial letters of the words 'Mi Kamoka Baalim Jehovah', which translates as 'Who among the mighty is like you, Jehovah?', the words spoken by Moses after the parting of the Red Sea, as reported in the book of Exodus. At the foot of the pillar are the words 'Leave thy fatherless children, I will preserve them alive, and let thy widows trust in me', a quotation from the book of the prophet Jeremiah.

The pedestal of the column has a poem from Lord Byron's 'Hebrew Melodies', beginning 'Oh! Weep for those that wept by Babel's stream'. This would have been very appropriate since the Molendinar Burn would have been flowing just a few feet away. On the left gatepost is another quotation from Jeremiah and on the right is one from Lamentations. The four religious quotes are from books that are part of both the Jewish Torah and the Christian Bible.

The first burial here, which was also the first burial in the Necropolis, was that of **Joseph Levi** (1770–1832), a quill merchant who died in the cholera epidemic that swept through Glasgow in

1832. He was buried on 12 September 1832. There are a total of fifty-one burials in the Jewish cemetery, the last one made in 1851.

Now, note the two stones outside the wall of the cemetery, with inscriptions in both Hebrew and English. **Deborah Ascherson**, buried in 1847, and **Morris Isaac Rubens**, buried in 1851, were each in dispute with the leaders of the Jewish community when they died so they could not be buried in the communal ground. Their families did the best they could and buried them as close to the wall as possible.

There is a set of stairs to the right of the Jewish cemetery. Walk up these steps, then up two smaller sets of steps. Just ahead of you is a short wall, with a set of stairs to its left, just out of sight. If you're not totally confused by these directions, take these steps and turn into the second grassy path on the left. After about twenty yards, you will reach a tree and, just after the tree is a memorial to the Queen of the Gypsies, sadly minus its bronze profile. Unfortunately, nothing more is known about **Corlinda Lee** (d. 1900) than appears on this stone. The bare facts are that she was Queen of the Gypsies, that she married George Smith and that she died at 42 New

The monument to Corlinda Lee, Queen of the Gypsies.

City Road. Her character, however, is remembered in a few short lines:

> Her love for her children was great, and she was charitable to the poor.
> Wherever she pitched her tent, she was loved and respected by all.

Retrace your steps to the end of the grassy path, noting, on the left-hand side, the four matching memorials to Glasgow firefighters who died on duty and head for the top of the steps. Just to the left of the last few steps, five headstones along, is a gravestone with some appropriate lyrics and music – 'I know that my redeemer liveth.' After a bit of community singing (don't be shy, now), climb the final steps and turn right, past a line of graves, into a fairly big flat grassy space with paths going north and south.

Stop here to look round at the variety of monuments on display. If you face east (look towards the top of the hill), on your left is what is known as an Egyptian obelisk, which emerges straight out of the ground – rather than being placed on a base or pedestal, as the one you can see over your right shoulder is. This remembers **James Mackenzie** of Craig Park (1760–1838), one of the members of the Merchants' House who met in James Ewing's mansion in 1828 for the first discussions about creating this very cemetery. He was also Lord Provost of Glasgow in 1806–07.

Ahead, on the slope above the short wall, is one of the most important monuments in the Necropolis. Designed by Alexander 'Greek' Thomson, it is a highly stylised tomb chest and monument, derived fully from ancient Greek sources. It is dedicated to the memory of **Alexander Ogilvie Beattie** (d. 1858), the minister of St Vincent Street United Presbyterian Church, which was also designed by Thomson. Many of the architect's signature details are included here, including bands of repeating Greek design elements, the slight curve of the tapering column and the stretched-out urn.

Keep scanning to the right and you will see a square-shaped Greek monument, with four pillars and a flat roof. Below this lies **Hugh Cogan** (d. 1855), a Glasgow merchant and former Dean of Guild. The plain, unadorned monument was probably designed by J. T. Rochead. Further right are two columns, one channelled and with an urn on top and one plain but deliberately broken. The broken column, a Roman design, is used to indicate someone of great promise whose life and career were cut off in their prime.

As we scan the horizon further to the right, there is a Gothic pinnacle to **Mrs Lockhart** (d. 1842). It was designed by her brother and has carvings by John Mossman. So, in one sweep, we have seen Egyptian, Greek, Roman and Gothic monuments.

Now, turn to your right and head down the slope of the main carriageway, towards The Façade. As you descend, look to your left and you will see a touching statue of a weeping woman. Sadly, she appears to have been detached from the grave she was intended to grieve over.

Two of the earliest monuments in the cemetery were constructed in the section to your right, each in memory of members of the same family. George Milne, the first superintendent of the Necropolis, buried both his stepmother and his young son within a few months of each other. **Elizabeth Miles** (d. 1833), his stepmother, died three months before the Necropolis officially opened for business. **David Milne** (d. 1833), his four-year-old son, was buried in May of the same year and – unusually for the time –

was given his own headstone. This was paid for by an unnamed benefactor, who had been impressed by the service Milne had given to him following a bereavement of his own.

On the right, the last memorial before a path joins from the left is a monument to **Hugh Hamilton** (1791–1837), one of the few working men commemorated here. He was a cloth-lapper in a cotton mill and an orator in support of parliamentary reform, and the stone was placed here by the political organisation to which he belonged, the Glasgow Conservative Operatives' Association.

Just beyond this, on the right and in front of a hedge, is the monument to **William Miller** (1810–72), 'the laureate of the nursery', who gave us the immortal rhyme 'Wee Willie Winkie'. Miller was born in Glasgow and lived most of his life at 4 Ark Lane in Dennistoun, on the eastern edge of the Necropolis. However, when he died in 1872, sick and penniless, he was buried in the family plot in Tollcross burying ground. His friends and admirers soon founded a public subscription to build this handsome monument.

The poem 'Wee Willie Winkie' was first published in 1841 and is still going strong, being printed and reprinted in countries around the world – usually in

The monument to William Miller, author of
'Wee Willie Winkie'.

a form of Standard English, rather than the Scots of the original. It tells the story of Willie, a young town crier, who goes from house to house each night at 10 p.m., checking that children are in bed. The first verse, which is all that most people know, reads:

> Wee Willie Winkie rins through the toon,
> Up-stairs and doon-stairs, in his nicht-goon,
> Tirlin' at the window, cryin' at the lock,
> 'Are the weans in their bed, for it's now ten o'clock?'

The main character of the poem also gave his name to a short story by Rudyard Kipling, published in 1888, and, rather more oddly, to a Shirley Temple film made in 1937. In the film, Shirley turns transvestite and joins the British army as a soldier called William Winkie, nickname Wee Willie. Moving swiftly on . . .

7

THE BODYSNATCHER AND THE BREWER

IN THIS CHAPTER, we'll travel from a maker of children's rhymes, via a potter and a policeman, to one of the best-known brewers in Scotland.

Leaving the father of Wee Willie Winkie behind, head south again and take the rather grand avenue that passes behind The Façade. To the right, next to a small tree, is the family grave of the Thomsons, the most famous of whom became better known as **Lord Kelvin** (1824–1907).

William Thomson was born in Belfast in 1824, the fourth child of a family of seven. Headed by James Thomson, a mathematics lecturer, the family moved to Glasgow, where the father taught and the son enrolled as a student at the university. By the age of twenty-two, William was professor of natural philosophy (that is, physics) and well on the way to a marvellous career as a pioneering scientist. He made advances in thermodynamics, mathematics, electromagnetism and hydrodynamics. He also designed the scientific underpinnings of the first transatlantic cable, for which he was knighted in 1866. The only stain on his science jotter was his opposition to Charles Darwin's theory of evolution. He was buried in Westminster Abbey but is remembered here on the family gravestone.

A small point, but most people who are elevated to the peerage derive their title from their surname and the name of a place they have strong associations with (Lord Scott of Gilshochill has a certain ring to it, don't you think?). Thomson, however, became Baron Kelvin of Largs, combining the name of the river that flowed past his place of work with the name of the town nearest Netherhall, his country estate. He probably should have been Baron Thomson of Netherhall but there you go.

On the left is an amazing series of tombs that become grander as we pass along. The best ones are, in order of walking past them: **William York** (1799–1865), a builder – look out for the bronze detailing; **John Macfarlane** (d. 1869), professor of medicine at Glasgow University; **John Bell** (1765–1842), owner of the Glasgow Pottery – note the great Egyptian doorway designed by J. T. Rochead; and

James Dunlop of Tolcross (*sic*) (1818–53). At the end of the row of monuments, with their backs to the wall, is the outstanding Grecian monument to **Esther Cooper** (d. 1851), daughter of Henry Ritchie Cooper of Ballindalloch, which has to feature one of the finest pieces of figurative sculpture in the Necropolis and which would stand its own against anything in Kelvingrove. The two angels, carved by John and possibly George Mossman, may represent Hope and Resignation. The phrase 'the face of an angel' could have been coined for the figure on the left.

Then we have a rather odd grotto. It was hacked out of solid rock and, just to make sure everyone knew it had been hacked out of solid rock, it was lined with a volcanic rock called tufa, which signalled to people who were fluent in the language of gardening that this was meant to represent a grotto hacked out of solid rock. Why can you never find a semiologist when you need one? (That's someone who studies the meaning of signs and symbols in human communication, for those of you who were off school that day.) The grotto belongs to the linked Higginbotham and Bolton families. **Samuel Higginbotham** (1798–1881) was an important cotton manufacturer in Glasgow.

The lettering on the last monument on the right in the family compound is oddly reminiscent of fridge magnets. Next, we come to the impressive family plot of the Pattison family, many of whom were soldiers. To the left of the family burial ground is a monument to Lieutenant **Alexander Hope Pattison** (1813–34) of the Second West India Regiment, who died and was buried in the Bahamas. The monument is a solid block that supports a sculpted pile of military gear, including a helmet and a sword. On the right is a massive square column, topped by a full-length statue of Lieutenant-Colonel **Alexander Hope Pattison** (1787–1835), uncle of the person of the same name on the left and commander-in-chief of the Second West India Regiment. He also died in the Bahamas. The monument, by John Ritchie, includes the names of his various victories against Napoleon. Note the detail on the front of the monument – a butterfly encircled by a serpent holding its tail in its mouth, two powerful symbols of rebirth and immortality. Both Alexanders were buried in the same tomb in New Providence on the island of Nassau.

One member of the family, however, made his name in another profession. **Granville Sharp Pattison** (1791–1851), brother of the commander-in-chief, was an anatomist and surgeon and he became one of four defendants in the only trial in Scotland of members of the medical profession for grave-robbing. In 1813, he was accused, along with his partner in the College Street Medical School and two of their students, of removing the body of Janet McAllaster from the Ramshorn churchyard in Glasgow. The trial, which was held in Edinburgh in 1814, ended with not proven verdicts for Pattison and his student and the others were found not guilty. He later left Scotland and founded departments of anatomy in London and New York. He was also one of the founders of Baltimore Infirmary. His name, complete with spelling mistake – Granville Sharpe Pattison (a misplaced 'e' at the end of Sharp) – is on the right-hand stone of two matching memorials with freshly painted family crests on them.

Follow this path as it leaves the original area of the Necropolis and heads down into what had been the quarry. Just before the path levels out, there is a short set of steps to your left. Go up the steps and take the left of the two paths that appear. In a few yards, you will see, to your left, a rare item – a gravestone designed by Charles Rennie Mackintosh. The stone, the earliest recorded commission by the young architect, remembers **Alexander McCall** (1836–88), for eighteen years the chief constable of the Glasgow police. Mackintosh's father was a policeman, too, so he may have got this piece of work through family connections. Generally, the grey granite Iona cross is easy to spot but it has been pushed over at least twice and, at the time of writing, was lying face down and in two pieces. Apart from the Glasgow Style lettering on the bronze panel, which includes a profile of McCall by James Pittendrigh Macgillivray, there is nothing particularly Mackintosh about the monument.

From here, navigate towards the figure of John Knox, which you can see above the quarry face in the upper Necropolis. Head for the set of stairs that climb the quarry face. But, before we climb the stairs, there are a couple of items worth a look. To the left of the area where the stairs are, there is a rather dilapidated Gothic monument, to the memory of **Alexander Mackenzie** (d. 1875), a Glasgow merchant. Unusually, this is made of cast iron and a distinct lack of maintenance has allowed the Glasgow weather to slowly turn it into rust – ashes to ashes, rust to rust, perhaps. The monument was made at the Sun Foundry by George Smith and

The gravestone of Alexander McCall, designed by a very young
Charles Rennie Mackintosh.

Company. To the left of the metal pinnacle is a very similar monument in stone.

To the right of the stairs are two monuments belonging to the Tennent family, one to **Hugh Tennent** (1780–1864) and one to his son **Charles Stuart Parker Tennent** (1817–64). In 1886, the book *Memoirs and Portraits of 100 Glasgow Men* described the brewery that father and son had developed from a small family business to an international concern:

> The brewery is one of the most interesting sights in Glasgow. But it is not only a brewery, it is a maltster's, a cooperage, an engineer's shop, a printing office, a wright's yard, a saw mill, a carriers' quarter, for nearly everything required in the business, except the bottles, is made on the premises, which extend to over 10 acres ... The firm brew annually over 4.5 million gallons, of which one third is stout. Two thirds of this is exported chiefly in bottle, and the Messrs. Tennent, though not the largest brewers, are the largest exporters of bottled beer in the world.

As you climb the stairs, have a close look at the modern brewery and the face of the quarry. You can see how the whinstone is cracked and easily broken. This made it unsuitable for constructing buildings or even tombstones but it was used in making roads all through the city. So just as the Necropolis holds the remains of people from all over Glasgow, the main roads in and out of the city all have some of the Necropolis in them.

At the top of the stairs, take a moment to enjoy the view over the city. At least you can tell people that's what you're doing while you get your breath back.

8
IT'S ALL GREEK TO ME

NOW WE HAVE REGAINED the moral high ground, let's take a lofty look at some of the founders of the Necropolis, as well as a Polish freedom fighter, Glasgow's first artistic sculptor and a nautical author whose words are still inspiring young sailors today.

From the top of the stairs, turn left to visit the mausoleum of Major **Archibald Douglas Monteath** (d. 1842), one of the largest and most decorated monuments in the Necropolis. It was designed by David Cousin of Cousin and Gale in a richly detailed Romanesque style and was based on the circular Templar church of St Sepulchre in Cambridge. Around the door and below the eaves are a choir of grotesque faces and the frame around each niched window (now beautifully concreted up) is different.

Monteath was an officer in the service of the East India Company and, when he died, he left £1,000 to be spent on this monument, a phenomenal sum for the time. He shares the mausoleum, which is ten metres in diameter, with his brother **James Monteath Douglas**, of Rosehall and Stonebyres (d. 1850), a partner in Hamilton, Monteath and Company, wine merchants. For the eagle-eyed reader who has just gone 'Wait a minute – Archibald Douglas Monteath and his brother James Monteath Douglas? What's the game with the names?', here's the explanation. Both were born Monteath but, in order for James to inherit money from a Douglas relative, he had to agree to having Douglas as his surname to ensure the survival of that branch of the Douglas family. Somewhat ironically, there is no mention of the names of either of the deceased or any other details, inside or outside this tomb.

If you stand with this round monument behind you, to your left is the monument to **James Buchanan of Dowanhill** (1756–1844). It is a structure that was designed after not one but two classical Greek monuments, piled one on top of the other. Downstairs is based on the Tower of the Winds at the Roman Agora in Athens and upstairs is a close copy of Athens' Choragic Monument of Lysicrates. This architectural novelty – from the drawing board of James Brown – may have drawn the attention of the winds, which blew the top part off in 1856.

The large circular mausoleum in the background is dedicated to two brothers, Archibald Douglas Monteath and James Monteath Douglas. The cylindrical monument in the middle ground is for James Buchanan.

Look towards the towering statue of John Knox on the summit of the Necropolis and you will see a roughly triangular piece of ground to the right of the path. The dominant monument is a statue to **William McGavin** (1773–1832), standing on an ornate scrolled base. McGavin, who was known as 'The Protestant' in a city of Protestants, was a bank manager and lay preacher. He published a variety of books and magazines that aggressively promoted the cause of reformed Christianity and his periodical *The Protestant* was, as Charles Rogers (the author of a comprehensive survey of Scottish monuments, *Monuments and Monumental Inscriptions in Scotland*, written in the 1870s) rather mildly put it, 'devoted to the exposure of papal error'.

His monument was designed by John Bryce and executed by John Ritchie. The statue was carved by Robert Forrest, who also made the statue of John Knox at the top of the hill. James Berry described the architectural mode as 'early Victorian baroque with mixtures of Flemish and Elizabethan styles'. McGavin was buried in the crypt of Wellington Street Church and this monument was erected by public subscription. When the church was demolished to make way for the Alhambra Theatre, the contents of the crypt were reburied in the Necropolis so McGavin and his monument are now at least in the same graveyard.

Browse the triangle and keep an eye out for the very fine carving of a mourning angel, supporting herself on an inverted torch. Then there is a memorial to, among others, **Eliza Jane Aikman** (1852–1929), who founded the Glasgow Infant Health Visitors Association in 1908. Next is the imposing domed Roman Doric monument to **William Dunn of Duntocher** (1770–1849), engineer and cotton manufacturer, designed by J. T. Rochead. After that is the family monument of **Peter Mackenzie** (1799–1875), a radical journalist and publisher of the *Glasgow Reformers' Gazette*. And finally the grave of **Joseph F. Comozynski** (d. 1845), a Polish freedom fighter who 'died in exile at Greenock'.

Take a moment to find an almost hidden terrace, belonging to two families with strong connections to the Necropolis. On the west side of the triangle, there is a path that slopes down to the south. Go down this until you are beneath the double-decker Buchanan of Dowanhill monument and then turn right down a grass path to a secluded corner. Here you will find some of the descendents of James Ewing, one of the founders of the Necropolis.

Humphry Ewing Crum Ewing Junior (d. 1878) died on the family estate in Demerara, now part of Guyana, where rum, sugar and spices were produced and shipped home to Glasgow. When he died, he was placed in a lead-lined coffin, which was filled with rum to preserve the body on the long journey from South America to the very spot where you are standing now. Next to him is **Walter Ewing** (d. 1882), another family member, who died in Calcutta. Presumably, he was curried and delivered back home.

If you are feeling fit, climb over the low wall or follow the path back and round to the other side of the wall. You will now be in the semicircular family plot belonging to **Laurence Hill** (1791–1872), another of the founders of the Necropolis. Hill, a solicitor, acted as collector of the Merchants' House, factor of Glasgow University, clerk to the Faculty of Physicians and Surgeons and as secretary to many other Glasgow organisations.

As a businessman, he was involved in the Garnkirk to Glasgow railway line and in the first attempt to create a railway between Glasgow and

Edinburgh. He was a prime mover in creating the Necropolis and also the later Sighthill Cemetery, the first in Glasgow to be promoted by a joint stock company.

Barbara Hopkirk (d. 1833), Hill's first wife, was the first person buried in this compartment and one of the earliest people to be interred in the Necropolis. George Blair, writing in 1857, was slightly more specific, regarding her as 'the first Christian lady, moving in the upper or respectable ranks, whose remains were deposited in the cemetery'. She died of debility, at the young age of forty, after producing thirteen children.

This terrace burying ground, with its great view over the city, originally had cast-iron gates at each end. These are gone now and there isn't much left of the neat balustrade either. Sadly, this has become the public bar of the Necropolis – at least if you're fourteen and pretend to like the taste of cider. The tracery of the gates was formed from the letters of two pieces of poetry. The south gate was decorated with three verses of Logan's 'Paraphrases' and the north with a stanza from the poem 'Minstrel' by James Beattie. The balustrade along the western front was originally topped by four vases. Nowadays, it's empty vodka bottles – that's postmodernism for you.

As you head north out of the hillside terrace, take the path that begins with a few steps and rejoin the main walkway. Immediately ahead of you, it splits into two, one slightly to the left sloping down to the main carriageway and a grassy one ahead that keeps to pretty much the same level. That's the one we're going to take but first look at the pedestal to your right, commemorating the sculptor **Peter Lawrence** (d. 1839). The pedestal is almost all that remains of what was one of the most exquisite monuments in the Necropolis, a weeping male angel carrying an upturned torch. The figure, carved by John Mossman in 1840, is long gone but a very fine profile of Lawrence by Mossman remains. The statue made Mossman's name as an artist, not just an artisan stonemason. The winged youth may have been intended to represent Thanatos, the Greek god of death. George Blair, writing in 1857, noted, 'The countenance of the figure expresses a subdued sadness, chastened by calm resignation, and mingled with that celestial beauty which points to a region of immortality and eternal youth.' They don't make them like that anymore.

Behind this is a Gothic pinnacle, commissioned by the lawyer **Matthew Montgomerie** (1783–1868) in memory of his wife. The structure was designed by Charles Wilson in 1842 in the style of a Decorated Gothic wall tomb and constructed by Hamilton and Miller. Two statues, which previously stood in niches on either side and are now sadly missing, represented Hope and Resignation. They were carved by John and George Mossman. The monument, which cost £400, was badly damaged by a fierce storm in 1856.

Taking the path ahead of us, you'll see that, just before the grand mausoleum, there is a rather odd structure, like a giant stone playpen. This is the burying ground that the Glasgow Dilettanti Society bought in 1835 and it was designed by David Hamilton, one of its members. The society was founded in 1824 to encourage the fine arts and its patrons organised annual art exhibitions in its premises in the Argyll Arcade. Two members of the society are buried here, apparently without any marker. They are **Andrew Henderson** (1783–1835), a portrait painter, and **Dr William Young**, a physician. They had been, respectively, the founding chairman and vice-chairman of the society.

Next is the largest mausoleum in the cemetery. It is dedicated to the memory of **John Aiken of Dalmoak** (1801–75) and his family and was designed by James Hamilton II in a Greek–Renaissance style. There are four vaults below, for different branches of the family.

Continue along the grassy path to almost the end of this section and then take the short flight of stairs on the left that go down on to the main path. Next to the stairs, facing the carriageway, is a simple memorial to **Michael Scott** (1789–1835), a Glasgow merchant with interests in the West Indies, where he had worked as a young man, managing a number of plantations. He was also the author of the nautical novels *Tom Cringle's Log* and *The Cruise of the Midge*. The first of these, regarded as a nautical classic, is still in print. It is set in the tempestuous world of the Caribbean in the early nineteenth century, where young Tom's progress through the naval ranks is beset by war, piracy, smuggling and slave-running. Samuel Taylor Coleridge thought the book 'most excellent'. Worse things happen at sea, we are told.

Now follow the wall on the right and turn into the carriageway that is most like a grand Victorian street. Its row of imposing mausoleums faces the city and looks like a terrace of architect-designed villas.

9
Ascending towards Heaven

In this chapter, we are travelling towards heaven, where the second highest hill in Glasgow meets the sky – with a little help from John Knox, the father of the Scottish Reformation.

Once we get going along this great Victorian drive, watch out for two of the classical symbols of death. On the left, on the first mausoleum, is a row of upside down laurel wreaths. In ancient Greece, the laurels were a symbol of victory. Inverted, they signalled death. Similarly, on the right, we will see a pair of inverted Roman torches. These are slightly more complicated. For the Romans, an upright torch, with a flame blazing away, was a symbol of life. Upturned and with the flame extinguished it, reasonably enough, indicated death. However, people in the modern world, who had a belief in life after death, inverted the torch but kept the flame.

On a more mundane note, keep an eye open for the drains, which were a novelty when the Necropolis was opened. Until then, no one had thought to drain the surface water from burying grounds. This alone would have made cemeteries much more pleasant places to visit, regardless of any public health benefits it might bring.

To the left at the start of this avenue, we have a rather odd door, seemingly cut into the rocky hill. This memorial commemorates **John Adam of Larchgrove** (d. 1874), proprietor of the Duke Street Pottery, who lies beneath the garden path, rather than behind the front door. The entrance presumably symbolises the portal between this world and the next one. Next door is a Greek Doric temple belonging to **Robert Black of Kelvingrove** (d. 1879). It was erected for his daughter Catherine who died aged twelve and it is probably the first mausoleum in the cemetery. The plaque inside shows that five of his children died before reaching their twenty-first birthdays.

Across the street is a small Tudor–Gothic temple to **William Motherwell** (1797–1835), a once-celebrated poet. He also laboured as deputy sheriff clerk of Renfrewshire, editor of the *Paisley Advertiser* and, later, as a very Tory editor of the *Glasgow Courier*. The monument and the panels illustrating some scenes from Motherwell's poems were designed and carved by James Fillans. There was originally a Parian marble bust of the poet, also from the hand of Fillans, in the central space of the monument. It was taken for safe-keeping, no doubt, by an art lover.

A little further along on the right, before a gap, we find **Professor James Jeffray** (1759–1848), professor of anatomy at Glasgow University all through the heyday of the grave robbers. He may never have taken a wooden spade to a grave himself but Jeffray was the principal beneficiary of all the bodysnatching that took place in Glasgow and the surrounding towns.

On the left, there are more mausoleums, belonging to the great and the good of Victorian Glasgow, some now sadly in need of much tender care. First up is **John King of Campsie and Levernholme** (1789–1875), proprietor of the Hurlet and Campsie Alum Works, near Barrhead, and the Cudbear Works in Glasgow. He was a director of the Merchants' House, the Chamber of Commerce and the Clydesdale Bank, the Forth and Clyde Canal and the Glasgow and South-Western Railway Company. His eldest daughter married Robert Stewart of

Murdostoun, the Glasgow Lord Provost who brought the city fresh water from Loch Katrine.

Second is the mausoleum of three sisters, **Margaret, Jane** and **Elizabeth** (d. 1875 – this is the only date of death given but it is known that Margaret and Jane predeceased her) **Buchanan** of Bellfield, near Kilmarnock. They were the daughters of **George Buchanan of Woodlands** (1755–1840), Glasgow. The monument, probably designed by John Stephen, was built and carved by the Mossman family of monumental masons and sculptors. The workmanship of the two draped urns, even though it is now partially obscured by layers of paint, is worth a close look. The sisters left £10,000 to the Merchants' House of Glasgow, on the condition that their tomb should be maintained in proper order and repair during all time coming. No comment.

Then comes a badly collapsed mausoleum for the **Hutchison** family. This structure, which would have been pretty imposing in its day, has a very interesting cast-iron frontage, which includes inverted torches and, for whatever reason, some rather fine Moorish screen-work in the centre gates.

The fourth mausoleum was built in a Tudor–Gothic style for **Angus Turner** (1801–76), a town clerk of Glasgow from the 1850s to 1872. He was widely disliked by the councillors – but then he was from Edinburgh.

Last on the left, before we reach the foothills of the John Knox monument, is the Egyptian Vaults, so named because it is Egyptian and it has vaults. These were designed by David Hamilton and built by the Merchants' House to temporarily house coffins of people whose graves were being dug or whose mausoleums were still being built. Shine a light into the darkness and you can see the passageways that go to left and right and the stone covers, with iron rings, of the individual vaults at ground level. All of this was excavated from the hill. The cast-iron gateway – which was made by Thomas Edrington and Sons – has three repeating panels, with inverted torches and laurel wreaths, those classical symbols of death. Above the gateway is an emblem of a winged hourglass, symbolising the rapid flight of time.

Now, go on to the flat path, with the triangle that we explored earlier to your middle right. At your right shoulder is a tall pink Peterhead granite obelisk to **Henry Monteith of Carstairs** (1765–1848), a manufacturer and dyer of cotton fabric. He was Lord Provost of Glasgow in 1814–15 and 1818–19 and a long-standing Member of Parliament for the city. He was also appointed Provincial Grand Master of Glasgow, a senior position in Freemasonry. Monteith, probably best known for the Turkey Red dying process, is buried elsewhere but his son erected this memorial where it would be seen by his peers.

Next to this is a marble bust, by John Mossman, of **Ralph Wardlaw** (1779–1883), regarded as one of the finest preachers of his day. His church stood at the corner of West George Street and Dundas Street, a site that is now host to a non-smoking pub. Aye, progress is a fine thing.

To your left and a few steps to the east is a magnificent monument to **John Henry Alexander** (1807–51), a hugely popular actor and manager of the Theatre Royal in Dunlop Street (for his epitaph, *see* p. 115). The names of the architect (James Hamilton) and sculptor (Alexander Handyside Ritchie) are clearly inscribed on the monument, which is in a baroque style. The figures of comedy and tragedy flank an empty stage that is complete with footlights and the other carvings refer to the various props you might expect to see on the tragic or comic stage – all very theatrical, daahling. Alexander's family, incidentally, get less than top billing – their names are round the back.

To the right is a colossal white marble bust, by James Fillans, of **Dugald Moore** (1805–41), a literary bookseller and poet who wrote the once-famous 'The Bard of the North' and 'Midnight in Glencoe'. The second one sounds like an exceptionally low-budget horror movie or perhaps some Scottish supermarket's own brand of perfume.

Now we're ready to make the trip to the top – the nearest point to heaven. As you start to climb the grassy slope to the summit, take a look at four monuments to religious men. First, on the left, is the circular monument to **Dr John Dick** (1764–1833), minister of Greyfriars United Presbyterian Church in Albion Street and professor of theology to the United Secession Synod. Dick died in 1833 and was buried in the Cathedral burying ground. This monument to him, designed by Robert Black, was raised five years later by his congregation. It was, like the upper part of James Buchanan of Dowanhill's monument, loosely based on the Choragic Monument of Lysicrates in Athens. There was once a vase in the centre of the memorial.

Second, at centre left and looking like a blackened church spire, is the monument to the preacher

This magnificent monument is dedicated to John Henry Alexander, actor and theatre manager.

Duncan Macfarlan (1771–1857), designed by J. A. Bell in the High Gothic style. Macfarlan became principal of Glasgow University in 1823 and minister of the Cathedral the following year. He was also twice moderator of the General Assembly of the Church of Scotland and he spoke at the laying of the foundation stone of the Bridge of Sighs in 1833. Macfarlan's likeness can be seen halfway up the monument in a bronze profile by William Brodie.

Third, on the right, is the whitish Portland stone monument, designed by John T. Emmett of London, to **William Black** (1801–51), minister of the Barony Church. This Gothic antique, which originally had a canopy over the reclining figure of Pastor Black, complete with a scaled-down version of his own church, would look at home inside a medieval church. However, out in the bracing air of the Necropolis, it is much easier to see the four panels, which tell the story of the death and resurrection of Jesus Christ. Pay special attention to the risen Christ, powerfully bursting open the door of his tomb and scattering a group of Roman soldiers. Now pay very special attention to the poor soul trapped under the door.

Fourth, on the far right, is the monument to **Robert Muter** (1771–1842), minister of Duke Street

United Associate Congregation. The monument was designed by John Stephen in a vaguely Greek Doric style with ornaments from a variety of sources. It occupies a site that had been chosen by Muter because he could look to the east and see his house, Broompark. This much-decorated tomb has a solid base, with a sarcophagus surrounded by four pillars and topped with a fancy lid.

So who had the power and authority, not to mention chutzpah, to claim the burying place closest to Knox? **James Ewing of Strathleven** (1775–1853), one of the founders of the Necropolis, that's who. Ewing was a leading West India merchant and held most of the leading roles in Glasgow society at various times, having been Lord Provost, Member of Parliament and Dean of Guild of the Merchants' House. He also served on the committees of a number of philanthropic organisations, including the Glasgow Infant School Society and the Glasgow Royal Infirmary.

Ewing's mansion was on the site where Queen Street railway station now stands and he made a pretty penny selling his house and gardens to the Edinburgh and Glasgow Railway Company in 1838. He also had a summerhouse, first in Dunoon (now a museum) and then at Strathleven, near Renton in Dunbartonshire (now a business development centre). His monument, a sarcophagus of polished Peterhead granite, standing on a stepped pyramidal base of Aberdeen granite, was designed by the architect John Baird. Unfortunately, the years have taken away the bronze panels and friezes, which were designed by the Mossman family.

Now, the daddy of them all, **John Knox** (c. 1514–72), the 'chief instrument, under God, of the Reformation in Scotland', as it says on the base of his monument, which predates the Necropolis. A public subscription was raised to pay for the monument. Thomas Hamilton of Edinburgh designed the 18-metre-high fluted Doric column and the 3.6 metre statue of the reformer was designed by William Warren and sculpted by Robert Forrest. The whole edifice stands on the second-highest hill in Glasgow, which reaches 70 metres above sea level.

When the foundation stone was laid in 1825, thousands of people lined the streets and hung from windows to glimpse a grand parade going through the town on its way to the top of this hill and a reported 10,000 people crowded into the Cathedral churchyard to witness the ceremony. This was the

This fluted Doric column is the famous monument to John Knox.

first public statue in Scotland to Knox, who is buried in Parliament Square in Edinburgh – in a car park, at space number 23, apparently.

The people who raised the Knox monument have to be congratulated on their foresight. The reformer stands firmly with his back to Parkhead, home of Celtic Football Club, gazing fondly over towards Ibrox Stadium, home of Rangers. To be absolutely ecumenical, we should remember that Queen's Park play over towards the south and Partick Thistle to the north-west.

10
THE CLYDE BUILT MEN

THE FAMILIES OF THE GREAT INDUSTRIALISTS, the people who made Clydeside a world-famous byword for engineering excellence, are crowded into this part of the Necropolis.

Keeping John Knox on your left, head north, towards the huge, blocky new buildings belonging to the Royal Infirmary.

After a few yards, look over to the right, where there is a fine carving of a family of young children mourning the loss of their mother. There appears to be nothing to identify the family on the stone, which is certainly unusual. To the right is a double-decker monument to **Robert Stewart of Murdostoun** (1811–66), who was Lord Provost of Glasgow from 1851 to 1854 and who, if you remember, was responsible for introducing the supply of water from Loch Katrine to the city. The bottom half of his monument is Roman Doric and the top is Elizabethan in style. The lower section is derived from the

This carving depicts an unknown family of young children mourning the loss of their mother.

same classical monument that inspired the tomb of Sir John Soane, a London architect, which, in turn, influenced Giles Gilbert Scott when he was asked in 1924 to design the original red telephone box (ask your granny). The pioneer of clean piped water is also remembered by the Stewart Fountain in Kelvingrove Park.

Just ahead you will see a drunk man, exquisitely carved from white Cararra marble by Patric Park. Well, he's probably not supposed to look drunk but **Charles Tennant** (1768–1838) definitely has the air of a man who has just dropped both the glass and the bottle and is drifting off into an alcoholic stupor. All rather much for the inventor of a revolutionary way to bleach cotton and subsequently owner of the enormous St Rollox chemical works, the largest in Europe, which stood about half a mile north of here. It is perhaps ironic that the famously filthy fumes from his works are the main reason that the marble of the statue is gradually dissolving.

The much smaller monument on the right, a graceful obelisk of Aberdeen granite in memory of **Dr William Couper** (1757–1843), is so close to the pioneer chemist because three of his sons married three of Tennant's daughters. Note that the brewing family name ends in 'ent' and the chemical one in 'ant'. So watch the spelling the next time you're about to enjoy a pint of something with the name Tennent printed on the glass.

To the left of Tennant, in the row behind, is the tomb of **Alexander Fletcher** (d. 1845), a Glasgow flax spinner, reclining under a very close copy of the tomb of Scipio Barbatus (the Roman general who defeated the Etruscans) the original of which can still be seen in the Vatican Museum in Rome. It is in the form of a Roman altar and this example was designed by John Ritchie. Copies of the Roman original can be seen in just about every nineteenth-century cemetery in Europe. If you look closely around you here, you can see two more copies, in different materials and with slightly different details, but still recognisably the same design.

Continuing north along the path, we come to two of the finest mausoleums in the Necropolis. The one on the left, a Moorish kiosk designed by J. A. Bell, celebrates the memory of **Dr William Rae Wilson** (1772–1849), a noted traveller through Europe and the eastern Mediterranean. When Wilson's young wife Frances Phillips died just eighteen months after their marriage, he gave up his lawyer's office and

This extraordinary Moorish kiosk celebrates the life of traveller and author William Rae Wilson.

took to travelling and writing books based on his experiences. *Travels in Egypt and the Holy Land* was his best-selling book. Running to various editions, it inspired the theme for the extraordinary design of his monument, which must have seemed completely out of place in Presbyterian Scotland of that time. He eventually remarried a Miss Cates and she built this Saracenic marvel for him. Ramshorn burying ground in Ingram Street had previously been the chosen resting place for the Wilson family and being dead wasn't going to stop them enjoying the cachet of such a prestigious address. They were disinterred and joined their relative in his exotic mausoleum.

To the right is a rather angular Greek–Egyptian structure, commissioned in 1854 by **John Houldsworth** (1807–59) for his family, who were the kings of cotton. His father, Henry Houldsworth, had founded a cotton mill and foundry in Cheapside Street, Anderston, which prospered mightily. John went on to become the last Provost of Anderston. The mausoleum was designed by John Thomas, who also carved the three marble statues, which represent Faith, Hope and Charity, the three Christian virtues. On the left is Hope, recognisable by her symbolic anchor, and on the right is Charity, complete with babe in arms. Faith is inside, out of the rain, with a book. John Thomas was later put in change of the sculpture programme when the Houses of Parliament in London were rebuilt between 1835 and 1867 under Sir Charles Barry and A. W. N. Pugin.

Across the path and to the east of Houldsworth is **Alexander Baird of Auchmedden** (d. 1856), one of the Bairds of Gartsherrie, the family who rose to the top of the coal and iron industries in Scotland. Baird, who lies beneath a polished red granite version of the tomb of Scipio Barbatus, was Dean of Guild of the Merchants' House and he died in office in 1856.

A little to the north is an impressively large and solid monument, with an Aberdeen granite sarcophagus on the top. This one's dedicated to **James Sheridan Knowles** (1784–1862), an Irish actor and dramatist, who, at various points in his life, was also a soldier, a medical student, a schoolteacher, a lecturer, an elocution teacher and a Baptist preacher. On each corner of the monument, which was crafted by John Mossman, is a pair of sculptures showing the most celebrated characters from his dramas, including William Tell and Emma, from his 1825 drama *William Tell*. Next to him, in another circular monument inspired by the Choragic Monument of

Lysicrates in Athens, is **Charles Clark Mackirdy** (d. 1891). With its cast-iron door, the memorial was designed by James Thomson and sculpted by David Buchanan. Unfortunately, no one thought to mention what Mackirdy's claim to such an impressive burial place might have been.

Take the path between the cotton king and the old thespian. Ahead of you is a wall of stone with a semicircular top. This Edwardian baroque tomb commemorates **Walter Macfarlane** (1817–85) of the Saracen Foundry, whose cast-iron structures and details were exported around the world. The bronze portrait panel, with some fine art-nouveau details, is by Bertram MacKennal of London. Macfarlane started off in business in Saracen Head Lane, near the Saracen Head Inn, in 1850, before expanding into much larger premises in Possilpark. His impressive house in Park Circus is now the city council's venue for civil marriages. Oddly, there is no cast iron anywhere to be seen on the large granite tomb.

Opposite the king of cast iron is a modest monument to **Henry Dübs** (1816–76), an engineer who came from Germany and founded the Queen's Park Locomotive Works in Polmadie, which later merged with others to form the North British

Locomotive Works in Springburn, the largest in the world outside America. The enlarged company covered 60 acres, employed 7,500 people and supplied railways around the world.

Take the path to the right of Macfarlane and, after a few yards, you will come to another wall of stone, with what looks like an empty fireplace guarded by some pretty substantial bronze angels. This is the Allan family tomb and it boasts an impressive bronze inset by James Pittendrigh Macgillivray. **Alexander** (1780–1854) and **Jean Allan**, who founded the shipping dynasty represented here, were the subjects of the missing panel.

The Allan Line was one of the most important family shipping businesses of the nineteenth century and, at its height, it ran regular services across the Atlantic from Glasgow to as far north as Montreal and as far south as Buenos Aires. Alexander was a temperance campaigner so many of the family's ships were crewed by teetotallers and the only source of reading material on board warned of the dangers of the demon drink. Shiver me timbers!

Opposite this is a smaller monument to the memory of **David Edmund Outram** (1818–93). It is flanked by another pair of guardian angels. Outram was an accountant and the brother of George Outram, who edited the *Glasgow Herald* from 1837 to 1856.

Between here and the empty space to the east, have a wander among the graves and see what symbols you can spot on the stones. Among the monuments in this section is a slightly out-of-place pink granite enclosure, looking strikingly like an Egyptian bus shelter, which commemorates **John I. R. Grandison** (d. 1912). You will also find the grave of **Sir Hugh Reid** (1860–1935), who was in charge of the Hydepark locomotive works in Springburn, the district of Glasgow that became a world leader in designing and building steam locomotives. Also prominent is the freshly cleaned salmon-pink Celtic cross to the Campbell family.

Now head towards the open space to the east of this block of graves.

11
From Common Graves to the Royal Yacht

This part of the tour takes us from the common burial ground, past a poignant memorial to Glasgow's firefighters and on to the lower Necropolis, once a quarry whose output paved most of Glasgow's trunk roads.

As you cross the empty space, spare a thought for the thousands of people who were buried in communal graves here without headstones or any other markers. Make your way towards the left-hand end of the long row of parallel paths facing you, take the last full row from the left and pause around halfway along. On your right is a distinctive headstone, designed in 1910 by Talwyn Morris in the art-nouveau style for the **Blackie** publishing family. The firm was very well known for the fabulous artwork on its cloth-covered books, especially those for children. Morris, who was the head designer for

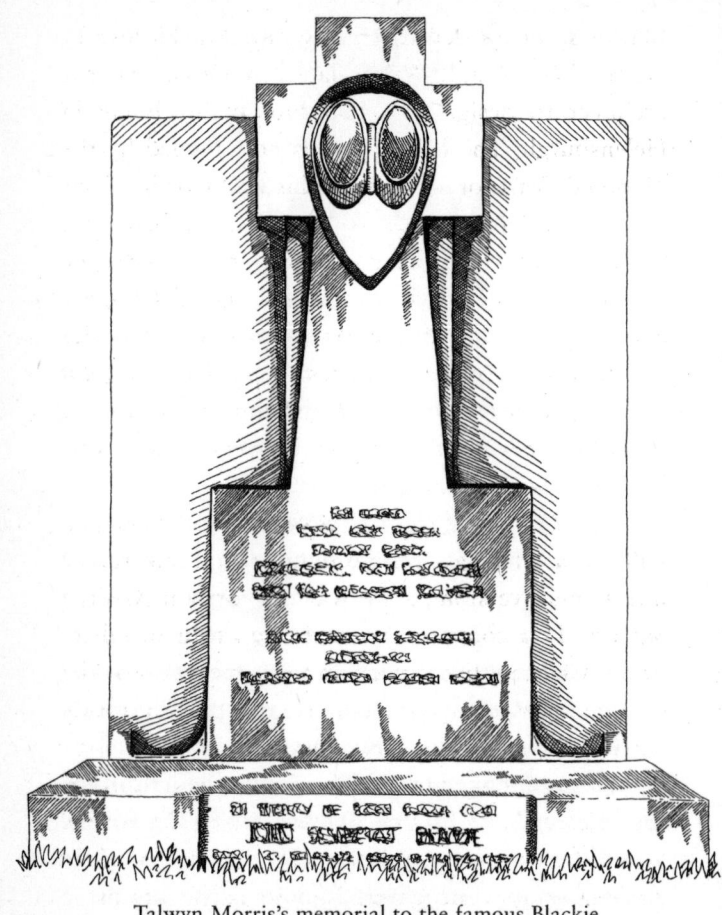

Talwyn Morris's memorial to the famous Blackie publishing family.

Blackie's, introduced Charles Rennie Mackintosh to Walter Blackie and Walter later commissioned the architect to design The Hill House, his home in Helensburgh. The Hill House is now owned by the National Trust for Scotland and is well worth a visit.

To the left of this is a scrolled tablet that commemorates the linked **Burns** and **MacBrayne** families, both of which owned well-known Glasgow and west-of-Scotland shipping companies. Opposite is a family grave that includes the remains of **John Glaister Junior** (1892–1971), Regius Professor of Forensic Medicine at Glasgow University, who was both an advocate and a doctor.

Squeeze through to the next row and here you will see a white granite monument, looking rather like a small version of the war memorial in George Square. This commemorates the fourteen members of the Glasgow fire service and five members of the salvage corps who lost their lives in the Cheapside Street fire in 1960. An inscription on the right side remembers the seven firefighters who were killed in the Kilbirnie Street fire in 1972. The Cheapside Street drama involved a fire in a whisky bond in Anderston and firefighters had to battle against a blaze fuelled by more than a million gallons of whisky and rum. An explosion inside the bond blew the walls of the warehouse out into both Cheapside Street and Warroch Street, killing nineteen of the 450 fire officers and men. On the other side of the river, twelve years later, a firefighter became trapped in a warehouse in Kilbirnie Street, Tradeston, and six of his colleagues died trying to rescue him. The fire was thought to have begun with an exploding light bulb. Relatives and others still place wreaths and flowers at the monument in the Necropolis on the anniversaries of these tragedies.

If you walk to the end of this row, you'll come to a low wall separating the summit of the Necropolis from what was a quarry below. We're going to take a short tour along the path next to the wall, before turning back to slip down to the quarry bed. If you have time, or perhaps on a second visit, you can explore the other rows of this large section, which hold many surprises and delights.

The graves at the end of each row, facing directly south over the city, were premium positions, so we can expect to see some big names. The first one of note is a squat monument to the professors of Glasgow University and their families who were buried at the Blackfriars Church, which stood immediately south of the university when they were both in High Street. The university stood on the east side of the street, opposite College Street, until it moved, lock, stock and test tube, to Gilmorehill in the west end in 1870. When the church was demolished in 1876, the contents of its graveyard were exhumed and reburied here. Some of the headstones were incorporated in the walls of the new building at Gilmorehill.

The second monument of note spreads itself out in an impressive fashion. It commemorates the **Stephens of Linthouse**, owners of an important shipbuilding yard immediately downstream of Govan. Alexander Stephens and Sons acquired the estate of Linthouse in 1869 and launched the first ship from the yard in the following year. The firm became famous around the world for designing and building cargo and passenger ships. Look out for the prows of Roman ships at the left- and right-hand edges and the Latin inscription (*vi et arte* – 'through strength and skill') around the oars on the central pillar. Those were the days, eh, when yard owners had imperial pretensions.

The simple granite monument to **John Strang** (1795–1863) belies his importance to the city. After travelling extensively through Europe, he became a journalist and poet, a translator of European literature and Glasgow's first art critic. He also founded the city's first daily newspaper. It had a very Glaswegian name – *The Day*. Later in life, he became City Chamberlain and his gift for European languages meant that he could conduct visiting dignitaries around the city in their native tongue. Among his publications were *Necropolis Glasguensis*, which became a kind of intellectual blueprint for the Necropolis, *Germany in 1831* and *Glasgow and its Clubs*. From around 1827, he promoted the idea of an ornamental cemetery for Glasgow in his journalism. He also ran the family wine-importing business, which gave him membership of the Merchants' House, and he was on the committee that oversaw the design and construction of the Necropolis.

During his last illness – or 'when the shadow had gone down upon the dial of life', as his biographer expressed it – Strang wrote to a friend whom he'd appointed executor:

> I should like my bones to be laid in the Glasgow Necropolis, in the establishment of which, it is well known, I took so active and so zealous a part. If the Merchants' House would grant me and my wife a small last resting place, as a recognition of my

> labours connected with the cemetery from 1827 to 1833, you will of course accept it – if not, you must purchase one.

The Merchants' House was happy to grant this wish and donated a prominent site at the end of a row, looking over the city that Strang had done so much to improve.

Up ahead is a rather fetching angel, perched atop the burying place of the **Whitelaw** family and keeping a close eye on the east end of the city, notably Celtic Park. This sculpture, who is obviously not a blue angel, is our turning point. Head back the way you came, following the quarry wall on your right.

In general, the grave markers in the quarry are from a more recent and less interesting age. However, as you take a right turn at the end of the wall and start your descent, look out for a heart-shaped monument, set in the ground, to **George Lennox Watson** (1851–1904), designer of the original Royal Yacht *Britannia*. The inscription ends with a motto probably understood only by naval architects – 'Justice to the line and equity to the plummet' – which makes them sound rather like sea-going Freemasons.

Follow the path down to the level floor of the quarry and then turn left. Just after the crossroads, on the left and opposite the grassy open area, is a monument to **William Dick** (d. 1880), the first secretary of the Scottish Football Association. The memorial was sculpted by George Galloway (no, not THAT one) and features the rather finely carved details of an old lace-up leather football.

12

ALL HUMAN LIFE IS HERE

THE FINAL PART OF OUR TOUR features a wide variety of people and monuments, from a Salvation Army bandmaster to a minor figure in one of the most celebrated court cases in Glasgow history.

Continuing along the same path, go through a small grassy gap on the left and immediately on the right is a well-designed and illustrated monument to Glasgow merchant **George Mason** (1838–1901) and his family. This imposing stone, which includes some rather fine Glasgow Style lettering and a bronze portrait by Archibald Macfarlane Shannan, has an odd red cast to it. The Mason family obviously had a few bob – and they were kind to their servants. How do we know that? Well, directly opposite their monument is a – naturally – smaller monument to the memory of their servant **Margaret McDougall** (1858–1904). To the right of the faithful servant's grave – which, rather unpleasantly, brings Greyfriars Bobby to mind – is another musical monument. The gravestone of **John Bell** (1823–56) features three bells (oh, my sides!), as well as the opening words and music of the song 'The Land of the Leal', taken from the works of Lady Nairne – all together now.

Go back to the path with the football administrator and on your right is another clear area where people were buried in common graves. Keep going, through a crossroads and towards a sharp corner where the brewery wall takes a sharp left turn. Just before the corner is a plaque on the wall. Oddly, it's not a grave marker but a reminder of a long-running boundary dispute between the Necropolis and the Tennent family.

Hugh Tennent, whose grave we passed earlier, took legal action against the Merchants' House, arguing that no graves should be dug in the lower part of the Necropolis because that was where he took his water supply for his brewery. If his rivals found out that his full-bodied beer with a good head on it was made with real bodies with real heads, he stated, he would lose all his customers. As the dispute rumbled on, the Merchants' House was careful to state its rights to the lands of the Necropolis so three plaques were placed in the southern boundary wall. The other two are either hidden behind banked soil or have been lost when the wall has been rebuilt. This one, with its rather precise measurements, is all that remains of the dispute.

From the boundary stone, head west for a few yards. To your right is an obelisk over the grave of **James Mitchell** (d. 1873), a prominent painter of his day. What makes this interesting is the inscription (*see* p. 8), explaining that his father and grandfather lived in a house on this very spot, which made it an ideal location for his last resting place. Continuing west from the painter's obelisk, there is a row of small stones on the left, on the bank of a slope leading down towards Ladywell Street. The fourth from the left was put up by the East Park Cottage Home and records a number of children and staff of this school for children and young people with special needs. There are more names on the back – quite moving.

Ten or so stones further along is another monument set up on a former family dwelling. It commemorates **Dr John Lauder** (d. 1847), a surgeon, buried on the site of his grandparents' cottage. Ahead of us now is a triangle with some trees and a few stones. There are two that always raise a laugh, an eyebrow or both. As you turn left into the path on the south of the triangle, look for a tall headstone to **Charles William Fry** (1838–82), the first bandmaster of the Salvation Army. You'll notice that he was born twice but died only once. On the opposite side of the path, a few steps along, is a modest stone in memory of **Archibald St Clair Ruthven**, a former Grand Master of the Texas Freemasons. It is, of course, a secret why he is buried here.

Actually, it tells you on the stone. Anyway, retrace your steps and join the main path that rises back up to The Façade. On your right, about halfway up the slope, is the lair of **William Harper Minnoch** (1820–83), the famous Glasgow … ehm, the famous Glasgow fiancé of Madeleine Smith. Smith, whose grandfather designed the Bridge of Sighs, was put on trial in 1857 for the murder of her lover, Pierre Emile L'Angelier, whom she was alleged to have poisoned with arsenic. The charge was found not proven but the steamy letters she had sent to her lover were read out in court and her reputation was ruined. She fled Scotland for London and later made a new life for herself in America. Minnoch was a director of Houldsworth and Company, a leading firm of cotton spinners in Glasgow. He doesn't seem to have been too traumatised by the trial of his ex-

The lair of William Minnoch, the erstwhile fiancé of the star of one of Glasgow's most notorious murder trials, Madeleine Smith.

fiancée for he married someone else less than a year later.

So we make our way to the turning circle in front of The Façade, and bid farewell to the city of the dead. Where Glasgow is still the Second City of the British Empire and where the merchant princes and other grandees of the past still slumber in imperial glory beneath Greek temples, Roman altars and Templar churches – not to mention Egyptian bus shelters.

13
THE WORDS AND THE STONES

PÈRE LACHAISE has a lot to answer for. The Parisian cemetery, probably most famous as the last resting place of James Douglas Morrison, lead singer of The Doors, also represents one of the most significant changes in commemoration and mourning of the dead. Unlike the pestiferous and bone-strewn churchyards and charnel houses that went before it, Père Lachaise was hygienic, was laid out like an aristocratic estate, had many architect-designed monuments and offered a pleasant and respectable space for people to contemplate the lives and deaths of their loved ones and indeed themselves. The makers of the Glasgow Necropolis wholeheartedly embraced this new model for creating an enlightened and ornamental cemetery.

Before Père Lachaise opened in 1804, gravestones and monuments looked death squarely in the face, in the form of perhaps the best-known funerary symbol of all, the skull and crossbones, which was often sculpted in perfect anatomical detail. This was a simple and direct reminder of death, of the end that meets us all, of the need to repent and secure a place in heaven. The Latin phrase that sometimes accompanies this symbol is just as straightforward, *Memento Mori* – remember death. Other grisly graphics included the Dance of Death, showing living people shimmying with skeletons.

As well as the death's head, with or without crossed femurs and sometimes even with wings, popular symbols on grave markers included: Death himself, the King of Terrors, portrayed as an erect skeleton holding the three weapons of death – the dart, the spear and the scythe or lance; the Angel of Death, shown as a chubby child carrying a dart, an hourglass or scales; the gravedigger's tools – the spade and the turf cutter or pick; and the hourglass itself, sometimes with wings. All of these are reminders of our mortality, of our eventual death and decay.

All this came to an end with the advent of Père Lachaise, which quickly became world famous and inspired similar garden cemeteries around the world. In the British Isles, these include Glasnevin in Dublin, the General Cemetery of All Souls, Kensal

Green in London and the Glasgow Necropolis. In North America, Mount Auburn in Boston opened in 1831, Laurel Hill in Philadelphia opened in 1835 and Green-Wood in Brooklyn opened in 1838 and all followed the fashion established in Paris. However, that new nation's monuments did tend to be smaller and less ornate than those of its European counterparts, reflecting the beliefs of its Puritan founders.

These modern cemeteries, following on from the French Enlightenment values that were turned to stone in Père Lachaise, turned their backs on the ghoulish and the ghastly, preferring the sober, cool and tasteful emblems of classical Greece and Rome. As well as borrowing complete monuments from that time period, the landscape gardeners, architects and monumental masons of the early nineteenth century who designed and furnished these new places of rest adopted the symbols and, in some ways at least, the outlook of these early civilisations.

In the Glasgow Necropolis, for example, there are monuments that are based on the following classical architectural structures: the Tower of the Winds in Athens (commemorating James Buchanan of Dowanhill); the sarcophagus of Cornelius Scipio Barbatus (there are several here and this design can also be seen in cemeteries of this period all across Europe and North America); the Erectheum in Athens (the Allan family, owners of a shipping line); and the Choragic Monument of Lysicrates (again, there are several of these, such as the memorial to Dr John Dick). There are also a number of tombs based on simple Greek or Roman temples.

The neoclassical motifs that replaced the death's heads and other macabre markings also showed a marked shift in attitudes to death. Those laid to rest in the gruesome graveyards of eighteenth-century Paris were damned to eternal suffering – in Père Lachaise, they were promised eternal sleep. Typical carvings on stones included flaming Roman torches, inverted to represent death, Greek laurel wreaths, winged Italianate cherubs, broken classical columns, Greek urns, draped or undraped, the Christian cross and a variety of borders and friezes taken from neoclassical architectural detailing. All of them were oblique, tasteful and respectable.

Following in this tradition, the modern cemeteries soon developed an array of familiar sculptural forms, such as statues of the deceased, angels standing guard over the tombs, weeping figures, often representing the bereaved, and, in some cultures, statues depicting religious characters, such as the crucified Christ or his mourning mother. Père Lachaise teems with eerie, shrouded, mourning figures, of which the best known is probably Madame Raspail, reaching into her husband's tomb for a final comforting touch.

This new, enlightened approach to death and the hereafter – which was thought of as a long sleep rather than an eternity of terrors – produced more cheerful symbols of resurrection and eternal life. These include: the winged soul, ascending to heaven; the Angel of the Resurrection, holding or blowing trumpets; the Radiance, represented by clouds, the sun, sunrays, trumpets or a sunburst; a flaming heart; palm fronds; an anchor; the Holy Spirit in the form of a dove; statues or carvings of Faith, Hope and Charity; a snake holding its tail in its mouth; the Agnus Dei or Lamb or God, seen holding a cross or flag; a phoenix rising from the ashes; and a pelican feeding its young with its own blood. All these can be found in the Glasgow Necropolis.

Philippe Aries, the great French historian of changing attitudes to death during the past 1,000 years, saw Père Lachaise and the reform movement that led to its opening as signalling a radical transformation in the way people saw death. He believed that the 'macabre iconography' of the Middle Ages had, in the modern world, transformed itself into an 'eloquent décor of death', becoming 'more distant and more dramatic' and honoured in elaborate Victorian funerals and mourning rituals. He also noted that, parallel to this, undertakers became more professional and started calling themselves funeral directors. All of this was mirrored in Glasgow.

If the French reformers who fashioned Père Lachaise intended to tame death and make it invisible, they failed in at least one important way. By making the cemetery more hygienic and pleasant and designed to promote mourning and silent contemplation, they invented the modern pastime of cemetery tourism. This, in turn, contributed to the Victorian cult of the dead, which remains with us today in popular pilgrimages to the graves of prominent people such as Jim Morrison.

FALLEN IS THE CURTAIN,
THE LAST SCENE IS O'ER,

THE FAVOURITE ACTOR
TREADS LIFE'S STAGE NO MORE.

OF LAVISH PLAUDITS
FROM THE CROWD HE DREW,

AND LAUGHING EYES
CONFESSED HIS HUMOUR TRUE,

HERE FOND AFFECTION
REARS ITS SCULPTED STONE,

FOR VIRTUES NOT ENACTED,
BUT HIS OWN.

(on the monument to John Henry Alexander,
actor and manager of the Theatre Royal,
Dunlop Street, Glasgow)

A Short Glossary

art nouveau – an architectural and design style, typically featuring flowing sinuous lines, entwined leaves and flowers, that flourished from the late 19th century into the early twentieth century.

baroque – an architectural style, featuring excessive decoration, use of large scale and curved forms, that flourished in the seventeenth and eighteenth centuries.

burying ground – a general term for a recognised place of burial.

cemetery – broadly, a designated place of burial not attached to a church. From the Greek for 'a dormitory or sleeping place'.

cenotaph – a memorial to someone buried elsewhere. From the Greek for 'an empty tomb'.

churchyard – a burying ground around or attached to a place of worship.

Elizabethan – an architectural style, featuring rich detail and symmetrical designs, that flourished in the late sixteenth and early seventeenth centuries.

Glasgow Style – a name for the Scottish interpretation of art nouveau that was popularised by Charles Rennie Mackintosh and his circle.

Gothic – an architectural style, featuring pointed arches and ribbed vaults and large windows, that flourished from the twelfth to the sixteenth centuries.

grave marker – a general term for headstones, memorials and other indicators that a dead person is buried nearby or a dead person is being remembered.

graveyard – any burying ground.

Jacobean – an architectural style, featuring a mixture of classical rustic forms, that flourished during the reign of James VI of Scotland (1567–1625) and I of England (1603–25).

mausoleum – a monumental tomb, generally an enclosed building that is decorated on the outside and has burial vaults beneath. Named after the burial place of Mausolus, a king of Caria, in Asia Minor, during the fifth century BCE.

memorial – a structure dedicated to the memory of a dead person or sometimes to remind people of an event.

monument – a statue, obelisk or other structure, designed to remind the viewer of a person or event.

Moorish – an architectural style, featuring horseshoe arches, geometric patterns, calligraphy and intricate detailing, derived from the Arab occupiers of Spain from 711 to 1492.

necropolis – a large cemetery belonging to a city in ancient times or a large modern cemetery, in the style of Père Lachaise in Paris. Greek for 'a city of the dead'.

neoclassical – an architectural style reflecting that of classical Greece and Rome.

Norman – the name for the **Romanesque** architectural style used in Norman Britain.

obelisk – a tapering shaft, square or rectangular in cross-section, usually erected as a monument.

Romanesque – an architectural style, featuring round arches, robust pillars and huge vaults, that flourished between the seventh and twelfth centuries.

A Short Glossary

sarcophagus – a stone coffin, often one decorated with a sculpture or bearing an inscription. From the Greek for 'flesh-eating' since the ancient Greeks made their coffins from limestone, which hastens decomposition.

sepulchre – a tomb, especially one in the form of a small room cut into rock where a dead person lies. From the Latin for 'a burial place'.

Tudor – an architectural style, also known as Perpendicular Gothic, featuring strong vertical lines, pinnacled towers and traceried windows, which flourished when the Tudors were on the English throne, from 1485 to 1603.

What Some of the Symbols Mean

anchor – deceased was a seafarer; the Christian symbol of hope and salvation.

anchor wrapped in vines – firm Christian faith.

angel, flying or with trumpet – resurrection.

angel, weeping – grief and mourning.

ankh – Egyptian symbol of life and immortality.

baby face with wings – often mistaken for a cherub, it actually symbolises the departure of the soul.

bird – the soul or spirit; resurrection.

broken column – a person, especially one of great promise, who died young.

butterfly – the soul or spirit; resurrection.

Celtic cross – the unity of heaven and earth.

Christian cross – death and resurrection.

What Some of the Symbols Mean

dawn – the rays of the sun represent resurrection, the triumph of day (life) over night (death).

door – the passage from this world to the next.

fleur-de-lis – the three prongs of this stylised lily represent the Holy Trinity.

garlands – victory in death.

grapes and grapevines – sacrifice.

handshake – farewell; friendship.

hourglass – a reminder of mortality.

hourglass, winged – a reminder that time flies.

ivy – immortality.

lamb – purity; innocence; sacrifice.

lamb and flag or cross – called Agnus Dei or Lamb of God, it symbolises Christ's sacrifice.

laurel leaves or wreath – earthly success; victory; immortality.

laurel wreath, inverted – death and resurrection.

palm branch – righteousness; resurrection; martyrdom.

pelican – the sacrifice of Christ on the cross.

pillar – in many traditions, tree of life, linking heaven and earth.

scales – justice; balance.

snake, biting its tail – rebirth; immortality.

snake, wrapped around a staff – called the caduceus, it is the symbol of medicine and is found on tombs of doctors and surgeons.

square and compass – Masonic symbol of judgement and geometry.

star – light overcoming darkness; enlightenment; wisdom.

sun, rising – resurrection; immortality.

torch, inverted – if not burning, death; if still burning, resurrection.

urn – mourning. (Draped indicates an older person, undraped indicates a younger one.)